Preface

CONSUMERS AND THE ECONOMY

This book is intended as a "polemical textbook", though the phrase may be regarded in some quarters as self-contradictory. It has been written in the belief that while existing textbooks of economics are quite adequate for conveying information and techniques of analysis, they do not equally successfully do what is the ostensible aim of most courses in social studies; induce students to think for themselves. Thus the book aims to introduce readers to some of the basic concepts, problems, and controversies of modern economics while at the same time putting forward some positive proposals for improving the position of consumers. As a supplement to existing textbooks it is hoped that it may be of use in general economic studies, approaching the subject from the standpoint of economic policy. More particularly it may be of use where an inter-disciplinary approach to social studies is being attempted, as a discussion of consumers necessarily involves crossing several disciplinary borderlines; in courses on liberal studies; in courses on comparative economic systems, for which the position of the consumer is a useful starting-point; and in courses of management studies, where it is sometimes overlooked that economic efficiency can be approached from the consumer's as well as the producer's side.

The book has been written over a period of six years. Chronologically, the first chapter to be drafted was Chapter 9, Scientific and Industrial Research and the Consumer. In the intervening period some progress has been made towards the policy objectives set out there, though a positive criterion for allocating research spending is still lacking. Another topic, the transition to the price mechanism in the Soviet economies (Chapter 3) was a subject of esoteric interest when the chapter was first drafted and is now common knowledge, but a discussion of centralized control of prices and production is increasingly relevant to Western countries trying to implement a prices-and-incomes policy.

The author is indebted to Mrs Christina Fulop; Mr Henry Smith of Ruskin College, Oxford; and Mr C. D. Harbury of the University of Birmingham for comments on early drafts of the book. Parts of the book have also been read by officials of the Consumers' Association and the International Organization of Consumer Unions. The author is of course solely responsible for any errors of fact or interpretation.

The author is also indebted to the following authors and publishers for permission to quote extracts from copyright material: J. S. Bain, *Barriers to New Competition* (Harvard University Press); Raymond Frost, *The Backward Society* (Longmans); Professor J. K. Galbraith, *A Theory of Price Control* (Harvard University Press); Eduard Heimann, *A History of Economic Doctrines* (Oxford University Press); Janos Kornai, *Overcentralization in Economic Administration* (translated by J. Knapp, Clarendon Press, Oxford); the executors of Ludwig von Mises, *Socialism* (translated by J. Kahane, Jonathan Cape); J. G. Morell, "Furniture for the Masses", *The Journal of Industrial Economics*, Volume V, No. 1 (Basil Blackwell); *Prices and Incomes Policy, Cmnd. 2639* (H.M.S.O.); and the October 1966 issue of *Motoring Which?* (Consumers' Association, 14 Buckingham Street, London, W.C.2).

Consumers and the Economy

Consumers
and the Economy

by

F. Knox, B.Sc. (Econ.)

GEORGE G. HARRAP & CO. LTD

London   Toronto   Wellington   Sydney

First published in Great Britain 1969
by GEORGE G. HARRAP & CO. LTD
182 High Holborn, London, W.C.1

© *F. Knox* 1969
Copyright.   All rights reserved
SBN 245 59671 2

Printed by
Cox & Wyman Ltd
London, Fakenham & Reading
Made in Great Britain

Contents

CHAPTER
1

Introductory

The rise of the "consumer movement" has been one of the most remarkable social developments in recent history. From Scandinavia and the U.S.A., where it originated in the inter-war years, it has now spread to almost all the developed countries of the world. A full history of the movement has yet to be written, as has an analysis of its aims, its problems, and achievements, and its place in the wider setting of economic and social policy. This book is intended as a contribution to the latter ends.

From the economist's standpoint, the consumer movement may be regarded partly as an instrument—one among very many—towards greater efficiency in the economic system. This is the standpoint adopted here; that is to say, the consumer movement is regarded as a means, not an end. No disparagement is thereby intended of the more usual approach, that of the promoters and members of consumer organizations, who have in the main been non-economists and who intend to help the individual to make the best use of his money, ignoring the effect on the economy. Economists for their part have tended to neglect the consumer movement, partly because of the normal time-lag between events and their impact on economic thinking, and, perhaps more important, the fact that the existing theory of consumers' behaviour, which occupies a substantial part of formal teaching of economics in Western countries, assumes perfect consumer knowledge and rationality. To admit "consumer protection" into the same arena of discussion would involve admitting that the assumption of perfect consumer knowledge has little basis in reality, and would lead to a degree of schizophrenia among both students and teachers.

Sociologists and political scientists might be expected to have more inherent sympathy for the subject but they could point out—with reason—that the logical place for discussion of consumers is in economics. Thus neglect of the consumer movement by the academic world, lawyers apart, has until recently been almost complete.

There is now hope that the situation will change; consumer questions
have come to occupy such an important part in public discussion
that they can no longer be altogether neglected, and as the traditional barriers between academic subjects are broken down (for
example, in courses in the newer British universities) it may be
expected that consumer questions will assume greater importance in
social studies.

Our subject-matter is the consumer interest and its promotion. No
serious problems arise in the definition of the "consumer". In practice, the main complication is the need to differentiate the final from
the intermediate consumer. Here (exceptionally) we may simply
adopt the verdict of the Molony Committee on Consumer Protection, the major official study of consumer questions which has been
made in Britain. "It was represented to us," the Committee noted,
"that the farmer, the small shopkeeper, the boarding-house pro-
prietor, and others in like case, purchase supplies and equipment for
business use on so limited a scale, and with so limited a business
experience, as to make their problems closely comparable with those
of the domestic consumer."[1] However, the Committee decided to
limit its inquiry to "goods acquired for private use or consumption".
A dividing-line must be drawn between the final consumer, buying
for himself and his/her household, and other consumers who buy
for re-sale. While their problems may overlap, and useful results may
be obtained by comparing their experiences, if action has to be taken
on behalf of the small-scale commercial buyer it is to his trade
organization rather than to consumer organizations that he must
look.

How to define the consumer's economic "interest" is open to more
debate. How far in fact do consumers and producers have conflicting economic interests, as workers and employers are believed to
do? How far can consumers themselves be said to have a collective interest? If a consumer interest or viewpoint exists, or should
exist, in what does it consist and how can it best be given
expression?

The classical economists originated the idea of conflicting interests, largely in connection with ownership of land, of which they
tended to take a jaundiced view. Owing to the pressure of rising
population on land, the landlord would wax fat without effort as

[1] Final Report of the Committee on Consumer Protection, Cmnd. 1781,
July 1962, para. 3.

society progressed. From the classical economists it was taken over by Marx, who postulated an inevitable conflict between workers and capitalists so long as the latter owned the means of production, with inevitable exploitation of the worker under capitalism. However, the conflict would vanish, with its expression, the State, when the stage of true Communism was reached. The reason for this is interesting and tends to be overlooked in political and economic analyses of Marxism: the conflict of interest would disappear because the division of labour which gave rise to it had disappeared. Under true Communism, "society regulates the general production and thus makes it possible for me to do one thing today and another tomorrow, to hunt in the morning, fish in the afternoon, rear cattle in the evening, criticize after dinner, just as I have a mind, without ever being hunter, fisherman, shepherd or critic."[2] (Marx, unlike some modern sociologists, would not have been perturbed by the "problem of leisure".)

The crux of the matter, from the point of view of the individual's specialization in production activity, is thus seen to be the rate of decline in working hours. For a variety of reasons, this has not so far progressed at anything like the rate which some prophets of automation predicted. However, it is reasonable to suppose that eventually it will reach the point at which the individual spends less than half his waking hours at organized work. It does not require any advanced economic or metaphysical theory to enable one to predict that eventually affluence may reach a point where few will be disposed to quarrel about economic rewards. Probably it is futile at present to attempt to predict when such a state of affairs will come to pass; if disarmament is achieved in advanced countries it might happen by the early or middle years of the next century. At the standard of living which will then prevail in advanced countries, at least those people who are prepared to limit their consumption demands may be able to hunt, fish, herd sheep, and criticize (or follow equally diversified unbucolic occupations) as envisaged by Marx. For present purposes, it need only be noted that even in countries with the highest standards of living there is little sign of this happening. So long as wants exceed production, conflicts of interest will remain.

The conflict of interests between workers and employers, like that between producers and consumers, arise, then, from the division of

[2] *The German Ideology*, Marx and Engels (Lawrence and Wishart, London, 1965), pp. 44-45.

labour. If all households produced all their own requirements neither of the two forms of conflict would exist. This is largely tautology, merely saying that if two classes of people did not exist they could not come into conflict. But it yields the important conclusion that so long as division of labour exists, so will conflicts of interest. The conflict between workers and capitalists is most simply seen in the division of profits between them; in the words of the Duchess in *Alice in Wonderland*, "The more there is of mine, the less there is of yours." (In games theory terms, the worker-capitalist relationship is assumed to be a zero-sum two-person game.) But the interests of worker and capitalist coincide in raising productivity, or at least can be made to do so if suitable means are found of linking increased productivity and wages, or by profit sharing.

In many ways what matters more than the *fact* of a conflict of economic interests is the way in which it is expressed. In Britain, as many strikes are caused by workers' grievances on non-wage subjects, especially arbitrary dismissals, as by wage demands. A legally obligatory appeals procedure for dismissals would therefore do as much as anything to reduce strikes. Many other strikes are due simply to a failure of communications between managers and workers, which, it may be hoped, will be substantially mitigated with progress in the social sciences and with improved management techniques. The point here is that while basic conflicts of interest are unavoidable, they are not necessarily sources of actual conflict. Strikes (the importance of which is in any case often exaggerated) are not primarily expressions of irreducible conflicts of interest but arise from other causes which can be dealt with by comparatively simple institutional measures.

The conflict of interest between producers and consumers over the division of the economic cake is analogous to that between workers and capitalists. Consumers are interested in low prices, sellers in high. The fact that this conflict of interest has not had the same degree of attention as that between workers and employers (and the fact that rising prices are not usually discussed in terms of a producer-consumer conflict of interests) may be attributed to the fact that wage negotiations occupy a central place in the industrial process while consumers' bargaining with producers over prices takes place continuously and in millions of different transactions.

The degree of conflict of interest between any individual producer and consumers as a whole depends on the former's efficiency. The interest of the consumer coincides with that of the producer who can reduce his costs and prices and thereby expand his share of the market. Here is the basis of the economist's predilection in favour of competition, and explains the central part which competition between producers has in economics.

While "workers" and "capitalists" are in the main mutually exclusive, "producers" and "consumers" overlap. More accurately, the class of producers is contained within the class of consumers. As Molony noted, the consumer is "everybody all the time",[3] but everyone is not a producer. "Pure" consumers are a heterogeneous group which includes the retired, the long-term sick, those too young to work, and others temporarily or permanently not working. (We assume for present purposes that housewives are productively employed.) Otherwise, the consumer-producer conflict might be said to be an internal one, between the individual in two different capacities. This is not unique to the consumer-producer relationship; some capital owners work, and some workers hold shares. However, the degree of overlap is considerably greater, and it follows from this (and also for other reasons) that concerted action by consumers on their own behalf is likely to be much more difficult than in the case of workers' organizations. But it does not in principle affect the definition of economic interest. Another analogy is the conflict of interest between motorists and pedestrians. Everyone is at some time a pedestrian, while motorists are a limited group, but this does not prevent the conflict between them being carried on in the bitterest terms.

While no producer can entirely neglect his interest as a consumer, his interest as a producer must normally take precedence. A worker in the shoe industry might expect a rise in his wages to result in a rise in the retail price of shoes, but these form only a small part of his expenditure on consumer goods, and it would be irrational for him to desist from his wage claim solely because the price of shoes might go up. For this reason, appeals and exhortations to workers to limit their wage claims in order to stabilize the cost of living are unlikely to have much success.

The consumer interest is in this book interpreted mainly in terms of prices. To a large extent, this is merely a convenient shorthand.

[3] Final report of the Committee on Consumer Protection, para. 16. However, not quite "all the time". We later draw a distinction between the interest of the individual as a consumer, and his interest as a citizen. The consumer is the citizen when he is spending money.

Certainly "consumer satisfaction is not simply a question of price but of quality, design, fitness for purpose, convenience and after-sales service".[4] However, all these can in principle be translated into their price equivalent for the consumer. Price is a means of reducing to a common denominator all the factors which enter into consumer satisfaction. It is not always possible to make the transition in practice, as statisticians have found when trying to incorporate quality changes into price indices; in these cases suitable footnotes must be added to the statistics.

Delivery to the home is obviously equivalent to a price cut equal to the cost of travelling to the shop. This is an objective sum, being the same for each consumer using the same mode of transport. To it must be added the time and trouble of going shopping, a subjective factor which will vary from person to person. (Those who like shopping will not regard it as a cost but a positive utility.) The cost of after-sales service can easily be quantified and a high cost may be regarded as an addition to the initial price. It is reasonable to suppose that other aspects of quality can in principle be quantified and expressed in terms of their price equivalent, both for objective and subjective factors in quality. It is thus possible to adhere to our criterion of price as the simplest expression of consumer interest, while recognizing that consumer preferences are both varied and varying. Other things being equal, a price reduction benefits all consumers and a price increase harms them, and modifications due to quality improvements or deterioration can themselves be expressed in terms of prices.

It follows that, when we are considering policy measures to improve the position of the consumer, the objective must be to improve quality per unit of price. To neglect either price or quality is to make nonsense of most recommendations on consumer questions; if this sounds platitudinous it can only be said that it happens in practice all too often. The Molony Committee on Consumer Protection, in discussing the scope of its work, noted that "the question of price, not surprisingly, entered into a number of the recommendations made to us", but both those making the recommendations and the Committee itself appeared to believe that if it were to discuss prices it could only be with a view to recommending some form of official price control. After touching on some of the problems involved in price control it went on to say that it would regard

4 First (1963/4) Annual Report of the Consumer Council (H.M.S.O., London, 1964).

prices as outside its terms of reference.[5] In consequence, much of its discussions of quality, standards, etc., became as vague and unhelpful as such discussions usually are.

The same split often occurs in consumer complaints. In general, consumers are more prone to complain about quality, after-sales service, and so on than about prices, except after a sharp and sudden price increase from a level regarded as normal. For this reason, and also because a very high proportion (variously estimated at between a half and two-thirds[6]) of consumer complaints turn out to be unjustified, it is obviously necessary when considering action to be taken on behalf of the consumer to supplement information on consumer complaints with a considerable amount of "objective" information and as well as analysis of the consumer interest.[7] For this reason it is doubtful whether setting up a chain of complaints centres for consumers is the best way of using the limited volume of resources available for consumer protection work; pre-purchase information should probably figure far higher in the priorities.

Obviously, the aims of high quality and low prices may conflict. However, probably the most important single lesson to be derived from the experience of the comparative testing organizations in Britain and elsewhere is that paying a high price in itself provides no *guarantee* of high quality. In the absence of more objective information, consumers are well-nigh forced into accepting price itself as an indicator of quality, and probably nothing could contribute

[5] "But if the forces of free competition do not suffice to protect him from excessive or variable price, nothing less than price control will do." Molony Committee, Final Report, para. 6.

[6] The main source of statistical information on consumer complaints in Britain is the Retail Trading-Standards Association's "Trade Information Service" (available only to the trade). The R.T.-S.A. maintains a laboratory for testing, mainly of textiles, and will undertake testing for consumers on payment of an appropriate fee (normally about £3 to £5 for the kind of work it is asked to do). It claims that two-thirds of the complaints which it deals with are unjustified. The reason for this high percentage may be that the more obviously justified complaints are met by the retailer and do not reach the R.T.-S.A.

[7] In 1965 the Consumer Council carried out a survey on the safety of young children by asking mothers what they *believed* to be the most dangerous items in the home. On this kind of question consumers' *opinions* are largely irrelevant; what is needed is a technical-statistical survey of accidents and their causes. The Consumer Council seems to have fallen victim to the fallacy, prevalent in "pop sociology" circles, that surveys of opinion are more scientific than other kinds of research (p. 30, 1964/5 Annual Report of the Consumer Council).

more to promoting the efficiency of competition than to impress firmly in consumers' minds that the link is by no means automatic. Both manufacturers and retailers usually have an interest in persuading consumers to spend as much as possible on their product (though retailers will, subject to profit margins being similar, sometimes provide objective information on the merits of competing products) and will therefore try to propagate the notion that price is a good indication of quality. The argument that high prices are necessary (and, it is often implied, sufficient) to ensure high quality is frequently brought forward in support of further bogus claims— e.g., that resale price maintenance is needed to ensure after-sales service.

Since quality can in principle be translated into its price equivalent, it simplifies matters to interpret the consumer interest in terms of prices, and to discuss measures for strengthening the position of consumers mainly in terms of their ability to offer resistance to price increases. The qualification "quality being unchanged" and the corollary that an improvement in quality is equivalent to a price cut should be borne in mind. In general, strengthening consumers ability to resist price increases comes to the same thing as broadening the range of alternatives open to consumers, which is itself sometimes said to be the main aim of economic policy.[8] Consumers can reduce their purchases of products which have risen in price only if close substitutes are available which have not so risen. The criterion of resisting price increases also overlaps to a considerable extent the orthodox policy objective of strengthening competition, but goes considerably further. (Many liberal economists who regard this latter as the main desideratum would, for example, disagree with the emphasis in this book on consumer information.)

Nothing is to be found in the following chapters about doorstep hawkers of encyclopaedias, magazines, carpets, and fire-extinguishers, defaulting travel agents and estate agents, bogus charitable organizations, allegedly invisible deaf aids, or cures for baldness, rheumatism, dandruff, and the common cold. Nor is there anything about bait-advertising or switch-selling, or even such widespread deceptive practices as double-pricing (the practice of marking-down from a fictitiously high initial price which became illegal

[8] *E.g.* P. T. Bauer and B. S. Yamey, *The Economics of Undeveloped Countries* (Cambridge University Press, 1957), p. 149.

in Britain under the Trade Descriptions Act of 1968). Many of these may require legislation, though it is important to bear in mind, as is done in the Federal Trade Commission Act of 1914, that the variety of deceptive practices is almost unlimited, and that blanket legislation against deceptive practices may be better than *ad hoc* legislation to deal with particular abuses. In other cases the weapon of publicity may be adequate. Television, with its impact on the social groups most vulnerable to deceptive practices, provides a means of dealing rapidly with many of them—an opportunity which the medium on the whole has not been slow to grasp. The popular press has also long exercised commendable vigilance in this respect, even at times when its advertising revenue must have thereby been placed at risk. (Particularly worthy of mention is the John Hilton Bureau of the *News of the World*, which has been in existence since 1934.) However, as both trade and consumer organizations frequently point out, the shady fringes of any trade or industry are usually a small minority, and to concentrate the efforts of consumer organizations exclusively on these would be to neglect much larger problems. These larger problems concern the efficiency, not the honesty, of producers.

There is practically nothing about hire-purchase, that staple of works on consumer protection. The only *economic* issue of importance raised by hire-purchase, *from the standpoint of consumer interest*, is whether consumers are aware of the real rates of interest which they pay. There is evidence that they are not,[9] and a strong case for making it obligatory to reveal the real rate of interest to prospective borrowers. For consistency, this obligation would also have to apply to other forms of consumer credit—personal loans advertised by the banks in Britain some years ago at 6 per cent turn out to have a true rate of interest nearly twice as high if repaid at regular intervals. Given this information, the consumer could decide for himself whether to buy on hire-purchase; borrow from a bank, an insurance company, or another source; realize his savings; or defer the purchase until he can pay cash.

Four other topics, which it had been originally intended to deal with, have been omitted both to keep the book within reasonable size limits and because they are not very closely connected with its central theme.

[9] F. T. Juster and J. P. Shay, *Consumer sensitivity to finance rates: an empirical and analytical investigation* (National Bureau of Economic Research, New York, 1964).

B

This central theme, which is in no way original, may be termed the theory of the beneficial squeeze. Assuming at the outset that there are almost always methods by which businesses can increase their efficiency (though it is for the management, not consumers, to say how) the first arm of the squeeze consists of pressure by trade unions for higher wages. The second arm economists have generally assumed to be competition—if one firm raises its prices consumers will buy elsewhere. However, the evidence of recent years is that the second arm of the squeeze is too weak and needs to be strengthened. Many firms can and do raise their prices without losing sales (partly because other firms are raising their prices at the same time and the consumer in fact has no real alternative.)

The squeeze in this form can only operate if the businessman is left with no alternative but to increase his efficiency. It may be assumed that if he can evade it by cutting wages, he will do so. The strength of trade unions in modern industrial economies should normally be sufficient to prevent wage cutting, but it follows that price cuts brought about by severe deflationary policies and unemployment are not in fact helpful, since in conditions of severe unemployment entrepreneurs are able to cut wages, openly or otherwise. Nor does the squeeze operate if businessmen can evade it by means of subsidies, or protection against imports; nor, as has been indicated, does it work if they can automatically pass on cost increases to the public in the form of higher prices.

To return, the first of the four omissions is the scope and limitations of consumer research, especially motivational research. While market research is a great improvement on the hit-or-miss methods which prevailed earlier, it is essential both for consumers and for businesses in their own interest to realize that occasionally its results must be modified or ignored, for the same reasons as those mentioned earlier in discussing the limitations of consumers' complaints. Exclusive reliance on the findings of market research may lead to a position in which nearly all firms, for a time at least, are marketing identical products, and the consumer is thus deprived of genuine freedom of choice. Research having disclosed that green-packaged, menthol-flavoured cigarettes would be most likely to take the fancy of consumers, a situation arose in the U.S.A. where nearly all major brands produced became of this type. A more serious example: intensive research to find out what style of car would be most marketable led to the majority of models produced in the U.S.A. becoming almost indistinguishable for a period. Only when foreign "compact" cars began to make serious inroads in the American market did U.S. producers realize the potential for this kind of product.[10] Clearly there may be other cases in which producers have failed to meet a consumer demand *which it would have been in their own interests to meet*, owing to imitation of competitors and uncritical reliance on the findings of market research, or simply to lack of imagination. (The problem here is essentially that which faces the politician in deciding whether, and in what circumstances, to lead rather than to follow public opinion.)

The second omission is the housing problem, references to which will be found at various points in the book. Without doubt the failure of practically any country to solve the housing problem—with the possible exception of West Germany—is the most serious failure in economic policy from the consumers' point of view. Its omission is mainly due to the fact that it is too large a subject to deal with as an incidental to a discussion of consumer protection in the supply of other goods and services. Consumers' interests in house purchase are also rather more divergent than in other products; those who have in fact been able to secure enough capital to buy a house, especially in the south-east of England, at any time since the war have made an extremely good bargain, and the "consumer protection" aspect largely concerns those who have *not* been able to buy. It may be suspected that the intense discussion of such subjects as legal protection of house-buyers against minor defects in finish is out of proportion to the real problem; the basic problem is house prices. It is often said that the "quality" aspect of house purchase is of paramount importance in that, apart from the automobile, it is the only product where the consumer is likely to be involved in irreparable financial loss. Since houses are normally bought only once or twice in a lifetime, consumers have no chance of learning by experience. These arguments are not altogether convincing.[11] As noted, house purchase is almost invariably, in modern conditions, a very profitable investment, and there are already legal safeguards against serious defects such as structural inadequacies.

Thirdly, there is no discussion of the social services and the con-

---

[10] The cigarette and automobile examples in the U.S.A. are brilliantly analysed in Theodore Levitt, *Innovation in Marketing* (McGraw-Hill, 1962).
[11] It is also factually incorrect, in many cases, to say that houses and automobiles are the most expensive commodities bought by consumers. This distinction attaches to insurance policies.

sumer interest therein. This raises problems which go beyond those
of economic efficiency. (The author's view is that while there is a
pressing need to modify the social services to take account of the
interests of consumers, this is not in the main to be achieved by re-
verting to the use of the price mechanism. If so, a procedure for
ascertaining consumers' views and dealing with consumer complaints may be a high priority.)

The fourth omission is any sustained discussion of the consumer
interest in relation to the professions. This may be termed the "guild
problem"— *i.e.*, the problem of maintaining standards without restricting freedom of entry. Probably to a larger extent than is
generally recognized, it is the same problem as that of the consumer
interest in other spheres, and methods for dealing with it will have
to include consumer information (a *"Which?"* on the professions)
and measures against restrictive practices. Here we may remind our-
selves briefly of the case against restrictive practices in general. The
immediate effect is to raise prices, but more fundamentally they
limit entry into certain occupations, and by preventing the efficient
from expanding their share of the market, they prevent resources
being put to the best use. And manpower, it is often said, is our most
valuable economic resource. If this is true of manpower in industry,
it must be even more true of professional manpower, which is more
highly trained (though in terms of numbers involved industry is
more important).

It ought not to be taken as axiomatic that the public interest and
the consumer interest in all cases coincide (broadly, as has been
noted, the consumer is the citizen when he is spending money), nor
should it be assumed that if a conflict arises[12] the consumer interest
should necessarily take precedence. The needs of the domestic consumer and balance of payments considerations may conflict, though
it is argued in Chapter 2 that this conflict exists, if at all, only in

[12] Rather than saying that the consumer and the public interest may conflict
we might say that the consumer does not pay the full economic costs of his
consumption—*i.e.*, there are external diseconomies of consumption. This
argument is developed in E. J. Mishan, *The Costs of Economic Growth*
(Staples Press, 1967). The present author prefers the first approach, as the
economic value placed on such things as noise abatement and preservation
of the countryside or of historic cities is subjective, and will vary from person
to person. It therefore seems better to take the case for these causes out of
the economic sphere, and base it on non-economic criteria (though the policy
recommendations would be largely identical).

the short run. Much the same applies in the possible conflict between the needs of the consumer and the requirement of high investment to promote economic growth. A more serious potential conflict is exemplified in land and housing problems. The land problem is in Britain and in most other countries essentially a regional one, and in Britain could be alleviated considerably by abandoning town and country planning restrictions and utilizing for house-building most of the land area of South-east England. Few, it may be hoped, would support such a solution.

Many conflicts between the consumer and the public interest lie in the field of physical (or, as it is known in Britain, town and country) planning. A problem which is much in the public eye is the traffic problem in towns. To a considerable extent this arises from the failure to impose on the private motorist the (extremely heavy) economic cost of driving and parking in towns, but it may be that even if this were done private motorists would still wish to use their cars in cities to an extent which would involve radical and un- desirable changes in the cities' character. However, if the consumer is defined broadly enough, as the consumer of transport as a whole rather than the motorist, the presumed conflict disappears; it is also in the interest of transport users as a whole to restrict private motor- ing in cities. In other cases (though not in all) an apparent conflict between the consumer interest and the public interest will disappear if the consumer is defined broadly enough.

In accepting the case for more rapid economic growth, and in discussing how consumer pressure could further this aim, no judg- ment is intended as to the desirable allocation of resources between private and public consumption. To accept the case for growth does not necessarily imply that all the increase should be taken in the form of goods and services for private consumption; the increase could equally take the form of more public consumption or more leisure. These questions are outside the scope of the book. So is the question of how to raise the quality, in the non-economic sense, of consump- tion, a task which lies mainly with the educational system but which also places responsibilities on the media of mass communications.

Elaborating the argument that the price level is the most im- portant indicator of the strength or weakness of the consumer, it is argued (Chapter 2) that economic efficiency provides a case for strengthening the position of consumers. However, price stability achieved by legally enforced price controls is useless, if not actually harmful (Chapter 3). An analysis of the inherent limits on the economic power of producers, both political and economic, indicates other measures which are probably superfluous or undesirable. These include limitation on the size of firms, and on particular forms of competition. Also it is doubtful whether political representation of consumers as such can contribute very much, except in the crucial area of incomes policy (Chapters 4 and 5). In the remaining chapters, 6 to 12 inclusive, we attempt to identify areas of action and put forward some practical proposals for strengthening the position of consumers in the economy.

2

The Consumer in the Economy

In the economic order based on private ownership in the means of production no special institutions, such as political democracy has created for itself, are needed to obtain corresponding success. Free competition does all that is needed. All production must bend to the consumers' will. From the moment it fails to conform to the consumers' demands it becomes unprofitable. Thus free competition compels the obedience of the producer to the consumer's will and also, in case of need, the transfer of the means of production from the hands of those unwilling or unable to achieve what the consumer demands into the hands of those better able to direct production. The lord of production is the consumer. From this point of view the capitalist system is a democracy in which every penny represents a ballot paper. It is a democracy with an imperative and immediately revocable mandate to its deputies.

LUDWIG VON MISES[1]

The serf in modern society is the consumer.

AUBREY JONES
(Chairman of the Prices and Incomes Board)[2]

1. *The doctrine of consumers' sovereignty*

The idea that consumers are the supreme arbiters of what is produced under a system of free enterprise has a long and central place in the history of economic thought. It is set out, with varying qualifications, in most Western textbooks of economics, though probably few economists would adhere to quite so dogmatic a version as that quoted from von Mises in the passage above. It has to be sharply distinguished from the teleological version, that the consumer *should be* sovereign, which has an even older origin in Adam Smith

---

[1] *Socialism*, trans. J. Kahane (Jonathan Cape, London, 1936), p. 443.
[2] Speech on November 3rd, 1967, to the Consumer Assembly in London (organized to mark the tenth anniversary of the Consumers' Association).

without whose dictum "consumption is the true end and purpose of all production" no book on the political economy of consumers would be complete).

In its "positive" version, that consumers *are* in fact sovereign if the state does not intervene in the economy, or intervenes only to maintain law and order, prevent monopoly, and ensure stability of the overall price level by control of the money supply, the theory derives from two basic assumptions. These are that producers maximize their profits and consumers their satisfaction from a given income. Some difficulties have arisen in the interpretation of both these assumptions. Where the producer is concerned, much depends on the time-period over which the firm tries to maximize its profits, and the relevance of the maximum profits assumption to modern large-scale corporate enterprise, as distinct from the nineteenth-century owner-manager, has also been the subject of considerable debate. What is certain is that in a market economy a firm has at least to avoid making losses, and the maximum profits assumption is undoubtedly a useful first approximation to actual business behaviour. The assumption concerning consumers' behaviour raises more serious problems.

The theory originated in utilitarian philosophy, with which neoclassical economics was closely associated. Bentham's pain-pleasure calculus was taken over by F. Y. Edgeworth and elaborated in his book *Mathematical Psychics* published in 1881. The link between utilitarian philosophy and economics left economists rather out on a limb when the former became unfashionable, and economic theory was the target of attacks from sociological, philosophical, and ethical quarters. In the face of these attacks, economists tended to withdraw to an alternative position, in which the idea of the maximizing consumer was largely deprived of empirical content, and became in effect simply as assumption that consumers' preferences could be arranged in order.

While the tautological reformulation of consumers' behaviour is not entirely without its uses, some empirical content must be infused into it if it is to be of much practical explanatory or predictive value. This involves a return to a modified form of the utilitarian theory, as is recognized by Eduard Heimann:

> The traditional definition [of economic man] is: the man who strives for maximum satisfaction with minimum sacrifice. But this definition is trivial and tautological. . . . What is meant, then, by "satisfaction" in the definition of "economic man" is something

narrower; satisfaction as such, but a distinct kind of satisfaction; that which comes with the attainment of more goods rather than less. This restriction excludes the spendthrift as well as those who spurn the fruits of modern technology (*e.g.*, Gandhi) and the Nazis, who eschew economic intercourse, however profitable, with people whom they deem unworthy. Wherever such "extra economic" types of behaviour prevail, they prevent the adjustment of production to demand. In a free society the producer increases or decreases his output as the price of the product rises or falls in response to the fluctuations of demand. Thus, what is presupposed in such an economic system is a man motivated by a desire for a maximum quantitative return. This does not mean that the economic man must be an egoist, although he often is; the man who invests in his own business and the man in charge of a college or a hospital will both strive for a maximum quantitative return on the investment. What is important is that for the economic man quantitative considerations must prevail over traditional values or political passions.[3]

In practice, all that is needed for the price mechanism to work is that some producers and some consumers should react to a change in prices (either of factors of production or of the final product). That this will usually be so in the absence of obstacles such as ignorance and impediments to mobility can hardly be disputed.

If there is maximizing behaviour by producers and consumers, and if there is perfect competition (*i.e.*, no single producer is large enough in relation to the market to influence the price), then consumers' preferences will be satisfied within the limits of their incomes. Producers will employ factors of production in such a way as to equalize their marginal productivity and their price; any change in demand will make it profitable to re-allocate factors of production. In this way, an optimum allocation of resources is arrived at. Interestingly, in the prewar period a number of socialist economists took over the "optimum allocation of resources" approach and argued that only under socialism was precise allocation of resources in accordance with consumers' preferences possible, because of widespread monopoly in the capitalist countries.[4]

The theory can only indicate general trends, and whether and to what extent these trends operate in a given situation is a matter for empirical investigation. There are usually a number of factors which

[3] Eduard Heimann, *A History of Economic Doctrines* (Oxford University Press, 1945), pp. 73–74.
[4] See, for example, T. J. B. Hoff, *Economic Calculation in the Socialist Society* (Hodge, London, 1949).

make it difficult to assert that consumers' sovereignty prevails fully in any actual situation.

(1) While the theory assumes precise and conscious consumers' wants, most psychologists would hold that consumers' behaviour is considerably influenced by non-rational considerations. This is of course the foundation of most salesmanship, at least that directed to the final consumer. In addition the consumer's motivation may be sub-conscious, or different from the declared or ostensible motive.

(2) The theory assumes that consumers act as autonomous units, but it can be argued that consumers' preferences are in fact inter-dependent.

(3) Consumers, it is clear, are open to persuasion by producers. The most conspicuous method of persuasion is advertising, but on a more fundamental sociological plane it can be argued that the entire system of consumers' preferences is a consequence of the "state of production", a theory inherent in Marxism and recently re-stated in Professor J. K. Galbraith's book *The Affluent Society*.

(4) Consumers' preferences can be satisfied only within the limits of what producers decide to offer. A few economists (such as von Mises—see quotation at head of this chapter) would argue that the fact that producers do not find it profitable to market a certain pro-duct is in itself evidence that the product is not desired. However, unless there is some way of finding out how consumers would react to the presentation of non-existent alternatives, this argument is circular. As Maurice Dobb has said, "It may well be the case that the majority of the choices registered on the market are in fact second-best preferences as compared with the choices consumers would have made if the requisite alternatives had been available."[5] The question of whether and in what circumstances competition be-tween producers can lead to a reduction in the variety of choice (the best-known example probably is American television programmes) is of major importance, but is not discussed further in this book.

(5) The doctrine of consumers' sovereignty encounters some difficulties when a choice has to be made in allocating resources between present and future consumption. Some theorists hold that the problem is adequately dealt with by interest rates; this solution is not altogether convincing, and, rightly or wrongly, many govern-ments have decided that investment for future production (in which may be included education) should be higher than it would be if it was determined by individual rather than collective choice.

[5] *Political Economy and Capitalism* (Routledge, London, 1937), p. 311.

2. Consumers' sovereignty, efficiency, and growth

That "consumption is the sole end and purpose of all production" (the teleological version of consumers' sovereignty) can be inferred from a variety of philosophical assumptions. The simplest is no doubt that in economic as in other matters individuals should be allowed the maximum freedom, subject to restrictions designed to protect the freedom of others. It is not necessary to investigate the philosophical basis here, as there is every reason for accepting this simple formulation. However, some "liberal" economists who go further and claim that economic freedom is the basis of political freedom are on somewhat shakier ground if economic freedom is interpreted mainly in terms of freedom to spend one's income as one likes. As a basis for political freedom, freedom to choose one's place of residence and work, and a wide diffusion of capital ownership, are surely of greater importance.

Two objectives of economic policy which are often believed to conflict with consumers' sovereignty are (1) protecting the balance of payments, and (2) promoting economic growth.

Consumers in Britain were for many years not permitted to buy Australian wheat, Japanese cameras, and Californian tinned fruit because of the effect on the balance of payments. It is sometimes implied that a balance of payments surplus constitutes an objective of economic policy in its own right. However, a small degree of reflection and an acquaintance with elementary economics will show that this cannot be the case. The balance of payments assumes importance only because it has been one of the two major factors (the other one being price rises) which have forced most governments in industrial countries, and the British in particular, to restrict economic growth below the rate which could otherwise have been attained. The fact that at times most countries have been simultaneously worried about balance of payments problems (on a consistent definition of balance of payments surplus or deficit, an impossibility) raises questions which cannot be pursued here. It need only be pointed out that the argument concerns a possible conflict between consumers' sovereignty and economic growth, not consumers' sovereignty and the balance of payments.

Consumers' sovereignty might conflict with economic growth by diverting resources from investment to current consumption. To a certain extent, this conflict of objectives probably does exist, and its resolution is to some extent unavoidably a political one. However, on further examination the question becomes more complicated.

(1) There is now strong evidence that factors other than capital
investment account for the major part of economic growth. What
these factors are have not been adequately defined (this, indeed, is
the unsolved problem of economic growth). They certainly include
technical and scientific knowledge, entrepreneurial ability, economies
of large-scale production, and psychological and sociological features
which are both a cause and a consequence of economic growth, and
which result in a willingness to change traditional techniques, occupations, and locations. In the U.S.A. capital formation seems to
account for only some 10 to 15 per cent of the growth in Gross
National Product.[6]

Admittedly this way of stating the problem may be misleading;
even if capital formation is not statistically the major factor, it may
be a *necessary* factor in that other changes, such as technical progress, cannot take place without it. From this standpoint it might be
incorrect to talk of distinct factors of production. Capital investment and technical change, if unavoidably connected, should be regarded as a single factor. But much technical progress can be linked
to capital *replacement*, with no net new investment, and it is undoubtedly true that an increase in capital investment alone will not
bring higher growth, and it is very doubtful if, particularly in
advanced countries, a shortage of capital is a major hindrance to
economic progress. An example which might be quoted to the contrary is France; however, shortage of long-term investment capital
there is probably due mainly to a badly-organized capital market
and a xenophobic attitude to foreign investment.

(2) Even in underdeveloped countries, where some restriction of
consumption may be unavoidable to obtain resources for investment,
it tends to be forgotten that a project which brings a return in the
near future is, other things being equal, more useful than one which
brings a later return. This, coupled with the greater difficulties of
forecasting the longer-term future, should rule out massive forced
saving by taxation, inflation, or other measures.

In practice, however, the backward countries have a remarkable
preference for the sort of project yielding the slowest possible
return—the big construction project. Rather than trying to achieve
prosperity as rapidly as possible, they appear, incomprehensibly

[6] R. M. Solow concluded that of the productivity increase per man-hour
between 1909 and 1949 in the U.S.A., only 12·5 per cent was due to capital
investment ("Technical change and the aggregate production function",
Review of Economics and Statistics, August 1957).

enough, to be trying to delay its arrival as long as possible. . . . An investment project that starts to yield an annual return of £100,000 from today is worth over ten times more than an equivalent project that takes ten years to construct. The first project is bringing in an annual return over the ten years while the second remains under construction, earning nothing but still paying interest. On the national scale, this sort of difference is pretty significant for economic development. Part of every additional pound that the nation earns today can be saved and invested in additional projects. When investment produces quick results its beneficient effect becomes rapidly cumulative. But if there is a long delay before the first additional dollars come in, then the cumulative effect of investment is postponed. And in the business of economic development what is postponed may be lost for ever; for in the interval population grows and the demands of the people become more exacting.[7]

(3) It is impossible to make accurate forecasts of consumers' demand (domestic or foreign) and of supply (technological changes) for a long period ahead. Apart from questions such as population growth, the value of predictive studies declines sharply if the period of prediction is longer than five years, and forecasts for a period of longer than fifteen years should be treated with some degree of cynicism. Warning examples from the recent past include predictions of a permanent dollar shortage; of a long-term deterioration of the terms of trade of industrial countries *vis-à-vis* primary producing countries (expressed in the Paley Report in the U.S.A. in 1950 and in books such as Mr. C. A. R. Crosland's *Britain's Economic Problem* published in 1953); of a long-term fuel shortage due to exhaustion of mineral resources, particularly oil, which gave a stimulus to the British atomic energy programme; and of a long-term decline in population (based on the decline in birth-rates in the 1930's). More recently a very large increase in population has been forecast, based on the high birth-rates of the 1950's, which latter has itself had to be revised following a fall in birth-rates in the mid-1960's. Any investment programme, by a government or a private firm, designed to meet the postulated demands of the long-term future runs a serious risk of being wrong. If it is flexibly designed (*e.g.*, subject to annual revision) the investment is more likely to be profitable, and the possible conflict between investment and the needs of current consumption is considerably reduced.

[7] Raymond Frost, *The Backward Society* (Longmans, Green, London, 1962), p. 173.

3. *The consumer and productivity*

With a rapid rate of economic growth, measures could be devised to make price increases tolerable. Old-age pensions, the wages of lower-paid workers, sickness benefits, and so on could be tied to the cost of living. In the absence of measures of this kind, there is a strong social case for taking action against rising prices. Inflation, as is now generally recognized, hits hardest those who are least able to protect themselves—the groups mentioned, and workers who are unable to force their employers to pay higher wages, and are unable, for one reason or another, such as age or lack of skill, to change their employment.

The social argument concerns the benefits which would accrue to underprivileged groups as a result of resistance to price increases by the general body of consumers. It should not be confused with a parallel argument, which has much less validity, that the low income groups are most in need of "consumer protection" in the narrower sense, and of consumer education. It is true that for some goods and services, especially consumer credit, underprivileged groups pay more than others for the same, or inferior, products.[8] But in general the lowest income groups are under considerable pressure to make the best use (from their own individual standpoint) of their incomes, and it is quite clear that any substantial improvement in their position must come through an increase in their income, not through a better allocation of their expenditure.

The actual or potential effect of consumer behaviour on productivity also provides a case for improving the position of consumers in the economy. Before dealing with it, a brief conceptual discussion of productivity is called for. Like the largely interchangeable term "efficiency", the concept of productivity is one of the most widely used in economics but poses severe problems of definition, interpretation, and measurement.

The simplest measures of productivity—output per man-hour in physical terms, such as tons of coal or steel, or bushels of wheat—are of little use for policy purposes. The physical output of an American coal-miner may be higher than that of a British miner simply because coal in America is found in more accessible seams. In addition, if physical measurements are used it is impossible to

---

[8] See D. Caplovitz, *The Poor Pay More* (Free Press of Glencoe, 1963). Some economic justification for high consumer credit charges to the lowest income groups is to be found in the fact that they are necessarily bad credit risks, but this factor hardly accounts for credit charges as high as those prevailing.

make comparisons between different industries. Evidently a *value* measure is needed. Further, the value has to relate to total input, not simply to labour input, as labour output in the U.S.A. compared with Britain, or in oil refining compared with ship-building, or in one ship-building firm compared with another, may be higher because more capital is employed per unit of labour. But in a purely accounting sense all firms have equal inputs and outputs, in that all receipts are paid out to factors of production, and efficiency in this sense is always 100 per cent.

Profit per unit of capital employed is in many ways the best index of efficiency. One of the main problems with this index, or any value index, is that a firm which is not operating in a competitive environment can always raise the value of its output by raising prices. Because of this, the attempt to measure productivity must at present be admitted in some ways to be insoluble. In some cases, statistical measurement can be abandoned and a more pragmatic approach adopted. It can often be assumed, for example, that the relative rates of expansion of two competing firms provides a good indication of their relative efficiency. In firms or industries which export part of their production, the size or rate of expansion of exports is always a valuable indication, since monopoly power in export markets is very slight. (Efficiency, it is clear from the two latter examples, must include efficiency in selling.)

To the economic theorist, productivity consists in effective use of factors of production to satisfy consumers' wants. This raises again some of the quasi-philosophical questions touched on earlier in this chapter. As a practical measure of efficiency must include efficiency in selling as well as in production, it might be argued in some cases that the most efficient firms are engaged in modifying consumers' wants rather than in satisfying given wants. Even more important, the pure economists' criterion rules out any possibility of measuring productivity, since consumers' satisfaction cannot be measured, at least at present.

That this last point is not a purely philosophical one may be illustrated by an example from retailing. A department store could obtain a high rate of sales per employee by having only one sales assistant who rushed from floor to floor serving the customers. Similarly statistical output in retailing, in terms of sales per employee, per square foot of floor space, or per any other unit of input, could be raised by reducing the number of shops and making consumers travel farther for their purchases. So, with shortages and rationing, productivity in retailing as usually measured might show an increase. However, if there is competition and free consumer choice, a retail store which tried to raise productivity by these measures would soon lose its customers.

Assuming a competitive environment, the difficulties in measuring productivity—the fact that firms can raise the value of their output by raising prices, and the fact that consumers' satisfaction is subjective and unmeasurable—can to a large extent be ignored. In a competitive situation profitability, and even labour productivity if the comparison involves only one industry and the result can be shown not to be due to differences in capital employed, are useful measures of productivity. Such measures have formed the basis of the considerable amount of work on the subject done by the Anglo-American Council of Productivity (later re-named the British Productivity Council), the Organization for economic Co-operation and Development, and many other government and academic organizations. These studies have with one voice concluded that there are vast differences in productivity between the best and the worst, and often between the best and the average, firms in any given industry. It follows that very large economic gains would be realized if the performance of the average firms could be raised to somewhere near that of the best (or, more precisely, if the dispersion of firms around the average could be narrowed and the average raised at the same time).

In the blast-furnace industry in America,

> Average labour productivity is only approximately half best-practice productivity. If all plants were up to best-practice standards known and in use, labour productivity would have doubled immediately. In fact, a decade and a half elapsed before this occurred, and in the meantime the potential provided by best-productivity practice had more than doubled. This is not an isolated example; all the available evidence . . . points to the crucial importance of this delay in the utilization of new techniques.[9]

> The U.S. Secretary of Commerce . . . stated that the application of known modernization technology plus modern manufacturing techniques could raise the average overall U.S. manufacturing productivity by 10 per cent per annum during the next decade.

[9] W. E. G. Salter, *Productivity and Technical Change* (Cambridge University Press, 1966), pp. 6–7.

The wide disparity shown up by inter-firm comparisons, between the highest and the lowest rates of productivity to be found in each branch of industry gives a clear indication of what is possible.[10]

The same conclusion emerges from the reports of the Centre for Inter-firm Comparisons, an offshoot of the British Institute of Management. For example, one report by the Centre in 1964 showed "a fantastically wide range of profitability." Labour costs as a proportion of sales values were 50 per cent higher in some factories than in others in the same industry.

When Britain's industrial problems are being considered the same point is usually stated in the form that the most progressive British firms are the equal of any in the world, but the average are far below the best. This is indeed the outstanding cliché of booklets and talks on "What's wrong with the British economy" and of speakers at one-day conferences and business luncheons. There is every reason to suppose that it is true.

It is perhaps extraordinary, therefore, that little notice has been taken of the discrepancy between this conclusion and one of the most basic tenets of economic theory, that efficient firms will always expand at the expense of inefficient. If there are such startling differences in productivity why has not the normal process of competition remedied the situation by re-allocating market shares in favour of the efficient? Even if the re-allocation does tend to happen in the long run there is obviously considerable scope for improving efficiency and rates of economic progress by making it happen more rapidly.

Since little attention has been directed to the discrepancy, we cannot give a definitive explanation (nor, for present purposes, is one essential) but some tentative solutions may be offered. The normal obstacles to movement from one firm to another of factors of production, and from one product to another by consumers, are obviously a part of the explanation. Another possible explanation is that many firms do not in fact try to maximize their profits—and it may be that continual creeping inflation reduces the allocative efficiency of the price mechanism. Also, the efficient firm will expand at the expense of the inefficient only if it uses its superior productivity to cut prices, unless it can expand sales sufficiently by advertising. Whether the efficient producer will find it in his interests to cut

[10] O.E.C.D., *Productivity Measurement Review*, August 1964.

c

prices depends formally on the shape of his demand and supply curves, but there does not seem to be any clear and invariable reason why it should be in his interests to do so if he can reap the advantages of his greater efficiency in the form of higher profits per unit sold. He is benefiting the community by producing at lower cost (*i.e.*, using fewer resources per unit sold), but not benefiting it as much as he would if he cut his prices and increased his share of the market.[11]

Even if he does cut prices, he cannot be sure of an increased share of the market if there is consumer ignorance or inertia. The remedy must therefore be partly consumer information and education, a central part of what may be termed "consumer pressure". But to the extent that consumer pressure operates, it also solves the problem posed when the leader is for any reason unwilling to cut his prices. If there is effective downward pressure on prices by consumers (or, equally, pressure to prevent prices from rising) the firms at the bottom end of the efficiency scale will be put out of business and the efficient will therefore find themselves supplying a larger share of the market. The product will be supplied with a smaller total input of resources and the community will gain even if the efficient firm did not of its own volition cut prices.

Thus supporters of consumer protection (in the narrower and familiar sense, labelling, comparative testing, and action against deceptive practices) are right in a more fundamental way than they probably realize when they claim that the interests of the consumer coincide with those of the more efficient firms. The latter have much to gain and nothing to lose if the consumer's position is strengthened.

Gains in productivity which could result from an improvement in the position of consumers may be greater than the potential gains from productivity campaigns, if only because productivity "campaignology" has been intensively operated for a quarter of a century. It is in any case a truism that the firms most in need of productivity improvement are largely impervious to campaigns of this sort.

---

[11] The theoretical explanation may be that the "most efficient" firm would be subject to increasing costs if it expanded its output. This assumption has failed to find support in the empirical evidence—see, for example, J. Downie, *The Competitive Process* (Duckworth, 1958)—but it is important to bear in mind that the "most efficient" firm at one time may not be the most efficient at another (Marshall's "trees of the forest" analogy). However, so long as there are large differences in efficiency between firms in an industry at any one time, it must be true that there are potential gains to be derived from re-allocating demand and productive resources between firms.

That it is essential to re-allocate resources from the inefficient to the efficient more rapidly than the price mechanism, unaided, is likely to do, has become more widely appreciated. One possibility is a value-added tax, the only form of business taxation which varies proportionately to costs, and hence taxes firms in inverse proportion to their efficiency (in contrast to a profits tax, which taxes firms in direct proportion to their efficiency or a sales tax, which is efficiency-neutral). Another suggestion is that the results of inter-firm comparisons of productivity should be published with the names of the firms concerned. Hitherto, published inter-firm comparisons have taken pains to avoid any possibility of the firms concerned being identified. The argument is that shareholders and public opinion would then bring pressure to bear on the backward management to mend its ways. Like "consumer pressure", these proposals are a means of using *outside* forces to supplement the efforts of private and official management consultancy organizations to increase efficiency. The various possibilities are not, of course, mutually exclusive, but complementary.

3

Consumer Choice and the Price Mechanism

The survey reported demonstrates conclusively that consumers, under existing conditions, do not successfully safeguard their own interests. Moreover, producers apparently are not compelled, by an invisible hand or otherwise, to protect consumers either. Accordingly, the basic tenet of a free enterprise system— that consumers will direct production into channels that yield them maximum satisfaction—is hardly valid. Those who regard the potential benefits of free enterprise as exceeding those of other forms of economic organization would seem to be committed to provide a remedy for this deficiency.

A. R. OXENFELDT[1]

1. *Problems of the socialist consumer*

The theory that when goods and services are priced according to their costs of production, the price mechanism ensures that what is produced is best suited to what consumers want, has been set out, in rough and ready form, in the last chapter. This thesis, subject to varying qualifications, would be accepted by most economists in Western countries and is to an increasing extent being accepted by Marxist economists also.

From the middle of the 1950's, coincident with political de-Stalinization, rising living standards, and increasing contact with the outside world, a debate has been taking place among economists in the Soviet Union and Eastern Europe on the extent to which the price mechanism can be utilized in a socialist economy to bring about a more efficient allocation of productive resources and to make production accord more closely with consumers' demand. This change from previous economic policy may be interpreted to some extent in Marxist philosophical terms as a change in the ideological

---

[1] "Consumer Knowledge, its Measurement and Extent" (*Review of Economics and Statistics*, May 1950).

superstructure reflecting the increasing difficulty of guiding production in any other way once the standard of living has risen above the provision of basic necessities.

The lessons of the Soviet experience are similar to those derived by Western economists during the period of wartime and post-war controls, and provide a useful starting-point for a discussion of the price mechanism and consumers' choice, though familiar to most professional economists.

In Russia the debate on profitability and the price mechanism became general after September 1962. In that month Professor Lieberman of Kharkov University proposed in *Pravda* that a "reward fund" should be set up in every factory into which payments would be made according to the factory's profit on capital employed. Later in the year two other Soviet economists proposed a flat-rate charge of 10 per cent on capital, for which no charge had previously been made. In September 1965 the Soviet Communist Party's Central Committee adopted the "profit motive"—pricing according to scarcity and productivity for both capital and labour—as official policy. By mid-1967 it was estimated that 3600 enterprises, producing 26 per cent of the country's industrial output, were being run under the new system, including most of the output of foodstuffs, textiles, and other consumer goods, and several branches of machine production. These enterprises had been freed from the targets laid down in the general economic plan, allowed to decide their own purchases, and to decide the level and allocation of their "wage fund", previously laid down centrally.

Hungary introduced a "levy on investment capital" in January 1964 to be used as a guide to price changes in building, agriculture, food processing, and the wholesale and retail trade. Czechoslovakia followed suit a month later with a decision by the Government to "use price policy more effectively than hitherto as an important economic instrument with which to influence supply and demand". Prices of a wide range of goods in East Germany were raised in December 1964 with the intention of increasing incentives and taking account of charges for capital in the industries concerned. Then in January 1965 the Polish authorities announced that they intended to give more weight to profit as a test of efficiency. During the following years substantial progress was made towards allowing more scope for demand-responsive prices in all the countries of the Communist bloc except China and Albania. Jugoslavia, under its regimen of socialist competition, has had for many years flexible and frequently adjusted prices and interest rates; further liberalization measures, involving external devaluation and a sharp rise in the prices of domestic consumer goods as a stimulus to the producers, were put into force in 1966.

One of the earliest, and still probably the most fundamental, critiques of a centrally directed Communist economy from the standpoint of efficiency in the allocation of resources was written by a Hungarian economist, J. Kornai, in 1957.[2] The theme of the book is the impracticability of ensuring by central directive that what is produced conforms with what consumers want. Kornai also stressed the difficulty of persuading management to use its resources efficiently other than by financial incentives, and attacked the size of the bureaucracy needed to put these (redundant or harmful) directives into effect. In view of the paradoxical tendency in Western economies in recent years to revert to government control or supervision of individual firms and industries to try to prevent prices from increasing, a brief *résumé* of Kornai's analysis may not be out of place in a textbook on Western economies.

Under the unreconstructed system of Soviet planning, industries and firms were given production targets in advance for each year. These targets were based on known production capacity, though this is by no means a precise concept—it can usually be considerably increased by shift working—and production in the current year, generally with a percentage increase to fulfil the plan targets. The increase took account of the need to meet the overall plan targets; what the firm or industry would have to produce if suppliers and industrial customers were to meet *their* targets; and something akin to a market research forecast of changes in final consumer demand over the year. Obviously in these circumstances managers have every incentive to conceal their true production capacity in order to get their production targets fixed as low as possible, and to hoard factors of production in order to meet the expected increase in their output target as well as to allow for unforeseen difficulties. The central planners, well aware that plant managers are understating their capacity, in turn try to increase their targets.

Factory managers also have every incentive to insure against deficiencies in their factory or on the part of their suppliers by hoarding labour and asking for more (free) capital equipment for which they have no immediate need. A very similar situation prevailed

---

[2] *Overcentralisation in Economic Administration*, trans. J. Knapp, (Oxford University Press, 1959, published in Budapest in 1957).

during the Second World War in connection with spare parts for war equipment: "Over-insurance would lead to a surplus and waste of components; but such waste was never very obvious (on the contrary, many officials regarded the presence of large stocks of components as evidence of good planning), while the existence of a single aircraft without some necessary component was always sufficient to excite heated argument and discussion."[3]

Production targets may be fixed in terms of physical production (tons of coal, pairs of shoes); in terms of value of output; or in terms of value added. Each of these produces its own peculiar distortions. If the target is fixed in physical quantities it can most easily be met by producing cheap, possibly identical articles and disregarding any desire on the part of the consumer for variety or high quality (cf. the stories, not all of which appear to be allegorical, about Soviet shoe factories which met their production targets by producing only left or only right shoes). If the target is fixed in terms of the money value of output the factory finds its interest to lie in high-cost varieties and loses any incentive to keep down costs. If the target is fixed in terms of value added the firm has an incentive to concentrate on products which have the highest wages cost and the lowest proportion of "bought in" value (materials, components, and processes contracted out). In principle, a combination of targets might meet the problem—for example, high physical volume combined with high value added and low wages cost, but in practice such a target would be intolerably complex and it would be found that some of the objectives were inversely related to each other.

Once targets are set, there are many ways in which an alert management can raise its attainment figure, unhelpfully from the wider social standpoint.

In the leather trade, permitted outlays on wages and salaries are related to total production. If, therefore, enterprises run into trouble over these outlays towards the end of the plan period, the way out for them is to dump large amounts of raw hides into tanks for soaking. In an hour they can throw as much as two wagonfuls into their tanks and these hides immediately appear in total production as work in progress.[4]

It is also possible to raise production values simply by producing unnecessary products. All that is required for a product to be

[3] E. Devons, *Planning in Practice* (Cambridge University Press, 1950), p. 186.
[4] Kornai, *op. cit*, p. 39.

"reported finished" is that the factory MEO accept it, and that it be put in storage with other finished products. Whether consumers want the product or not is a matter of complete indifference from this point of view. If a product is later found to be faulty, or of poor quality, then a corresponding price reduction will be deducted from future production value at that time. But if the article happens not to be faulty (*i.e.*, is free from defects in materials and workmanship) and is nevertheless not wanted by anybody, then this has no consequences. It does not affect the fact that it will be credited as part of the "production value" credited to the enterprise concerned.[5]

It is very relevant to the concept of "countervailing power" (Chapters 5 and 6) that Kornai advocates measures which would increase the power to retailers *vis-à-vis* their suppliers as a means of checking the power of manufacturers to circumvent the spirit of the plan targets while adhering to the letter. However, to this end he advocates an increase in the volume of stocks held by the retail trade—a wasteful and expensive solution if any others are available.[6] A more promising line of approach is his suggestion that "commerce must also be in a position where it can provide industrial enterprises with financial incentives to satisfy the requirements of consumer demand to the greatest possible extent",[7] and he suggests that the prices payable to manufacturers by wholesalers and retailers should be varied according to whether orders are large or small, placed in good time or rush consignments, and so on.

Failure to adapt to consumer demand is reflected at the retail level by shortages (bath plugs and razor blades have been much noticed by tourists from the West), queues, or stockpiling of unwanted goods, though the last obviously encounters an upper limit in the willingness of retailers and wholesalers to hold stocks. A report in *Izvestia* (July 21st, 1964) reported the case of a small town which had been swamped with unwanted supplies of boots and caramels. When storage capacity reached its limit officials urged the factory not to send them any more but were told: "You must try to sell them. We cannot upset the factory's production plans."

The proportion of defective consumer goods has also been high

[5] Kornai, *op. cit.*, p. 38.

[6] "The distributive trades must be able to dispose of adequate stocks of finished goods, the possession of which is a condition of their being able to put up a successful fight in the interests of consumers." Kornai, *op. cit.*, p. 157.

[7] Kornai, *op. cit.*, p. 157.

enough to cause concern. The trade union newspaper *Trud* reported (November 22nd, 1964) that 20 per cent of the clothes, 10 per cent of the socks and stockings, and 9 per cent of the shoes reaching the shops were defective. Another feature of the retail and consumer goods sectors in the Soviet countries has been failure to introduce new techniques. In the autumn of 1966, with agricultural production in Russia expanding, it was reported that the collective farms were seriously hampered by the lack of food processing and cold storage facilities. A Russian periodical, discussing the advantages of pre-packing, pointed out that in 1958 only 4 per cent of the sugar, 5 per cent of the macaroni, 6 per cent of the salt, and 19 per cent of the confectionery sold in Russia was pre-packed.[8]

It is important to separate the questions of level of economic development (national product per head of population), the allocation of resources between civilian and non-civilian uses, and the allocation of resources available for civilian use between present and future consumption, from the questions which have been discussed above. The argument—as developed by internal critics—is that with a given volume of productive resources available for current civilian use, greater efficiency and consumer satisfaction could be obtained by making more use of the price mechanism.

2. *Price control*

The differences between the Soviet and Western types of economic system, it has frequently been remarked, can be exaggerated. Apart from the fact that in most Soviet countries a considerable volume of transactions take place outside the centrally planned exchange mechanism, the considerable part of the population in Western countries who are employed by central and local government is not subject to any market test of efficiency. The fact of operating in a competitive environment is of help, for example, in determining the salaries of civil servants, but the question of how to test the effectiveness of government spending and determine its optimum size and distribution is one for which no satisfactory solution has been found.

Most forms of government intervention, including taxation, may give rise to anomalies similar to those found in central planning. One example in Britain is purchase tax, leading to minute problems of definition. Commercial vehicles were taxed at a lower rate than private cars so that vans with side-windows were sold as commercial

[8] *Packaging in the Soviet Food Industry* (translated and reprinted by Joseph Crosfield and Sons, Warrington, 1963).

vehicles to people who wanted them for non-commercial use, until purchase tax was extended to vans with side-windows. Other purchase tax definitions were the subject of an entertaining Parliamentary campaign by Mr (now Sir) Gerald Nabarro, M.P., in 1958. However, all legislation involves problems of definition, which can be made to appear illogical, and the problems here relate to exceptions, not to the general rule.

A large private corporation in the West may resemble a centrally planned economy in its internal dealings. The national income of a small Soviet country such as Hungary may be less than the annual sales of General Motors, and, so the argument runs, should it not be possible to plan the Hungarian economy if General Motors can operate as a unitary organization? But a large Western corporation is subject in its external dealings to the market test of profitability, and if it is efficient will apply a market test to its internal operations —for example, if it manufactures components for its own use, by comparing their price with the price at which it could buy components from outside.

In wartime, however, the problems which arise in a capitalist country are exactly analagous to those which exist in a centrally planned economy, and a brief discussion of these is relevant for price supervision and control problems.

In Britain, price control effectively began with the 1941 Budget, when the Chancellor of the Exchequer, Sir Kingsley Wood, announced that the Government intended to stabilize the cost of living at the existing level, between 25 and 30 per cent higher than that of 1939. In April 1941 a system of price control was devised which was not finally dismantled until 1954.[9]

One problem immediately arising concerned the statistical index to be used. At the time the official index of retail prices was based on a Ministry of Labour family expenditure survey carried out in 1914. It was generally, and correctly, believed that the price of goods included in the index was kept down more than those of goods not included, so that the Government could point to its achievements in stabilizing "the" cost of living, particularly when negotiating with

[9] The British wartime price controls have been extensively documented and analysed, in official accounts and by academic economists who were employed in government service—e.g., J. Jewkes, *Ordeal by Planning* (Macmillan, 1948); L. Robbins, *The Economic Problem in Peace and War* (Macmillan, 1949); E. Devons, *Planning in Practice* (Cambridge University Press, 1950); D. N. Chester (ed.) *Lessons of the British War Economy* (Cambridge University Press, 1951).

trade unions. Candles, which were an important item of working-class expenditure in 1914, retained the weight in the index which they had in the expenditure survey of that year.

The Goods and Services (Price Control) Act of 1941 gave the Board of Trade power to fix maximum prices and margins for goods, and maximum charges for services. It did not specify the criteria to be used in fixing maximum prices, though in practice the Board of Trade had to use mainly profits, costs, and prices at the time price control was introduced.

The simplest form of price control is "cost plus", by which manufacturers are permitted to add a specified percentage of gross profit to their costs, and this initially formed the basis of most price controls in manufacturing. The problem immediately arising is that if manufacturers know that any increase in their costs will automatically be reflected in prices, and if a higher price is not likely to lead to a drop in sales (as is usually the case with shortages and rationing), they have no incentive to keep down costs. If profits are fixed as a percentage of costs rather than an absolute sum not only is the incentive to keep down costs diminished but there is a positive incentive to inflate them. Detailed accounting control over costs, such as is used in pricing government contracts in peace-time, cannot be extended to cover all industries owing to the amount of work involved, and even with government contracts in peace-time serious problems occasionally arise.

Price control depended on the application of fairly rigid quality specifications. When this was not done manufacturers could sell a lower-quality article at the controlled price of a better-quality one. In the event, this does not appear to have been one of the major problems of the wartime price control. The quality of foodstuffs is fairly standard and in any case closely controlled through the Food and Drugs legislation. In clothing and furniture, the price controls were backed by "Utility" specifications for a limited range of items of each product; the standardization and simplification thus achieved appears to have led to some improvement in productive efficiency. With products such as soap, tobacco, household utensils, household textiles, and pottery the scope for quality reduction, though greater than with food, is limited. The problem of induced quality deterioration is likely to occur mainly in consumer durables, which were not then a major item in consumers' expenditure and which in any case virtually ceased being produced as the engineering industries were converted to arms production; and in services—retailing, hairdressing, laundering, etc.—where a severe deterioration in quality is accepted as inevitable in wartime.

In other respects, however, problems did arise and on occasion became so serious as to make price control almost inoperative. When wholesale and retail margins are fixed as a percentage of the manufacturer's price there is a strong incentive to concentrate on the higher-priced products. There came about in consequence "the trading up characteristic of wartime—that is, the substitution of more expensive for cheaper articles. Manufacturers declared that they were continually being pressed by their wholesale and retail customers to charge more for their commodities, either by evasion of the price Orders or by the equally undesirable method of using more labour and materials per unit of commodity"[10] (a special case, from the distributive-trades aspect, of the problem of cost-plus pricing already mentioned). Where there was a second-hand market, enforcement of maximum prices for both second-hand and new products was often impossible, as an increasing proportion of the second-hand trade tended to flow through other than recognized dealers at uncontrolled prices. "In yet other cases dealers masqueraded as private persons in order to escape control."[11] The control of prices of second-hand goods had to be accompanied by control of charges for repair work, as repairs were often involved in a sale.

These controls can hardly have been very effective. Not only did the price of second-hand furniture continue to rise but the price situation became chaotic. There was often a wide range of selling prices for the same category of furniture, not only as between different shops in the same town, but even within a shop. It was common to find good furniture selling for less than bad, or, if at a higher price, for much less than was proportionate to its superior quality. Antique furniture had probably risen in price least of all. Mass-produced furniture, which was in greatest demand, had risen to three, four, five or six times its pre-war prices. One could not speak of a market but only of an unorganized welter of selling prices.[12]

Finally, it is clear that the size of the administration needed to enforce comprehensive price controls of this sort should be suffi-

---

[10] E. L. Hargreaves and M. M. Gowing, *Civil Industry and Trade*, (Official Histories of the Second World War) (H.M.S.O. and Longmans Green, 1952), p. 605.

[11] Hargraves and Gowing, *op. cit.*, p. 611.

[12] *op. cit.*, p. 611.

cient to rule it out in all normal circumstances. (One consequence is that the administrative work involved in making a price change is so large that prices are changed as seldom as possible, and when a change is made it is larger than immediately required in the hope that further changes will not be needed for some time.) As in Soviet micro-economic planning,

> It is no accident that the large-scale proliferation of the administrative apparatus should have coincided, in point of time, with the period under consideration here. The more instructions there are —particularly if they are of such a kind that there are no financial incentives, providing inducements towards their being carried out—the greater the need for reports, memoranda, local inspections, spot checks, and conferences. This in turn is inevitably accompanied by a growth of the bureaucratic apparatus at higher levels as well as within enterprises.[13]

Despite the problems which were encountered, it is feasible to argue that price control as practised in Britain and other major countries during the Second World War achieved its ends—*i.e.*, in stabilizing the cost of living and particularly in keeping down the price of essentials. However, this was done only with the help of accompanying fiscal measures, large-scale compulsory savings, rationing, and direction of labour; few economists would dispute that in these circumstances price control, for a time at least, can be successful. And in wartime price control and its accompaniments is almost universally accepted as both unavoidable and desirable, since the shift of resources to government consumption would otherwise lead to a totally unacceptable rise in prices and redistribution of incomes.

One economist who takes an unusually favourable view of price control during the Second World War is Professor Galbraith.[14] His thesis is worth mentioning as it bears on what comes later; in particular, it appears to be the origin of his theory of "administered prices" discussed in Chapter 4.

> It can hardly be argued that price control led to the kind of debacle that pre-war theory would have foretold. During the critical war years prices remained completely stable in the face of a large and continuing excess of aggregate demand over supply. Moreover, this stability was achieved, in considerable measure,

---

[13] Kornai, *op. cit.*, p. 114.

[14] *A Theory of Price Control* (Harvard University Press, 1952).

as the result of price-fixing *qua* price-fixing. . . . The entire weight of theory to the contrary, it had been proven possible to perpetuate, at least for a period of years, a disequilibrium at legislated prices . . .[15]

The explanation is a many-sided one. But the unifying core to which all or nearly all of the facets of the explanation are attached is the nature of the modern industrial market. These markets lend themselves to price regulation to a far greater extent than had previously been suspected.[16]

Galbraith divides the economy into two sectors: the competitive—mainly food and clothing—and the imperfect, where producers have a considerable amount of discretion over the prices which they fix. For price control to be successful,

> The steel, automotive, electric, chemical and like industries would have to be under price control, as would the wages of the unions with which these industries deal. On the other hand, prices in primary agricultural markets, clothing prices, and perhaps also margins for the generality of retail trade, would be left uncontrolled. Since they are demand-determined, and *if* demand is limited to available supply and is expected so to remain, they should show no tendency in the aggregate to rise. In this part of the economy, there is no built-in dynamic of price-cost movement even at full employment demand.[17]

Galbraith's recipe, therefore (produced mainly to deal with price rises brought about by the Korean War) is price control over prices and wages in the oligopolistic sector of the economy, and demands disinflation to maintain price stability elsewhere.

The theory is an attractive one but is open to criticism on several counts. First, to some extent it merely expresses the fact that price control is administratively easier in oligopolistic than in atomistic industries, reflecting in this respect the experience of the U.S. Office of Price Administration, in which Galbraith worked during the Second World War. "The great problems of price control", he notes, "have been encountered in food and clothing, the part of the economy which, with important exceptions, most closely approaches pure competition. At least two-thirds of the energies of the Office of Price Administration were devoted to these products and a con-

[15] *op. cit.*, p. 9.
[16] *op. cit.*, pp. 10–11.
[17] *op. cit.*, p. 71.

siderably larger portion of its failures were in this area."[18] (It may be noted in passing that the difficulties encountered in the U.S.A. in these product fields appear to have been due to a less efficient system of rationing than in Britain. For example the Department of Agriculture at times felt impelled to increase the quantity of rations for political reasons even though food supplies to meet the increase were not available.)

Secondly, in arguing that price control did not produce the expected side-effects—*i.e.,* it did not lead to a fall in the production of price-controlled goods—Galbraith appears to over-simplify grossly. He argued that controls during the period of the Korean War would not inhibit production, because during the Second World War "far more stringent controls had been consistent with the largest expansion in production in the nation's history."[19] This is to ignore the huge volume of unemployed resources in the U.S.A. at the outbreak of the Second World War.

Most important of all, however, his distinction between "administered" and other prices does not hold water, except for some limited validity in times of recession. This, however, deserves separate discussion in the context of monopoly (see Chapter 4).

3. *The scope for positive intervention*

It cannot be taken as axiomatic that lessons derived from centrally planned economies and from the war economies of the West are applicable to capitalist countries in peace-time. Price controls or the supervisory efforts of prices "watchdogs" are certainly unlikely to lead to severe shortages of the products concerned, if only because the controlled price would probably be raised as soon as a shortage became apparent. Neither can it be assumed that controls extending over only a few commodities, *and generally expected both by producers and consumers to be temporary,* will have the same effect as all-pervasive price controls over goods and services and factors of production, expected to stay in being for an indefinite period.

Nevertheless, it is much better established than most propositions in economics that if prices are fixed below the level which would have been reached otherwise, profits and wages in the price-controlled industry will be lower, and the quantity of labour and capital employed in the industry also lower, than they would otherwise have been.

[18] *op. cit.,* p. 26.
[19] *op. cit.,* p. 57.

Price control also reduces the effect of price increases in forcing consumers to look for substitutes and economize in the product which has risen in price—*e.g.*, to buy more mutton and less beef, or, if all meat rises in price, to increase consumption of fish. In advanced economies there is considerable scope for economy or substitution even of products which are traditionally regarded as "necessities". Thus, little progress was made in fuel economy in Britain, despite propaganda campaigns (directed mainly to industry) until after the mid-1950's, before which coal prices were held at an artificially low level. Use of water, quoted in textbooks as a commodity for which demand is absolutely inelastic (*i.e.*, it is a strict "necessity"), could be considerably reduced if it rose in price. It is no doubt true that drinking water is to a limited extent an absolute necessity, but this constitutes only a very small part of the total demand for water in a modern economy. Water for washing cars, sprinkling lawns, and sanitation could be economized by technical expedients. The scope for substitution is even greater as regards the industrial consumer of water, who can and does use considerable ingenuity in the search for substitutes for materials which have risen in price. In the example just quoted, the vast amounts of water used in industry for cooling purposes could, if water became more expensive, be economized by using the same water twice, by substituting air cooling for water cooling, and by other measures.

If prices are fixed below the equilibrium level it follows by definition that consumers will want to buy more than producers are willing to sell at that price. It may be admitted that there is rather more lack of precision about the concept of an equilibrium price than is allowed for in the textbooks, and that a price fixed only very slightly below the equilibrium may have no obvious side-effects. However, if the difference is large there is bound to be a discrepancy, which may be resolved by quality deterioration, rationing, black markets, queues, or subsidies. All have evident de-merits—rationing by queue, for example, is not likely to lead, in any sense, to a "socially desirable" allocation of resources since it is improbable that those who are able to spend most time queueing are the most worthy or productive members of the community.

Price control, as already remarked, tends to lead to a reduction in the supply of the controlled product, through a movement of labour and capital to uncontrolled industries, unless it is accompanied by direction of labour. Hence the familiar feature of suppressed inflation, with shortages of essential goods and ample supplies of non-essentials. Further, no matter what year is taken as the base date for the controlled price, changes in demand and supply conditions will make it obsolete and the planners will have little indication of what changes in supply and demand (particularly the latter) have taken place since control was established (though black market activities, if known, would provide a guide).

From these "basic platitudes" of economics, as Lord Robbins has called them, which are familiar to all those who have done the first year of an economics course—though apparently by no means familiar to politicians or the general public—economists have concluded that price control must be ineffective or harmful, or accompanied by measures unlikely to be accepted in a democracy in peace-time. In this they are correct. However, many have gone further and argued that there is nothing that governments can do to prevent prices from rising, other than by macro-economic measures, monopoly policy, and, some would now add, incomes policy. In this they are mistaken.

The correct conclusion is that if we want to prevent an increase in prices, we must do so by measures which do not interfere with the essential role of the price mechanism. If we want to stop a rise in the price of a particular product we must do so in the main either by increasing the supply of the product or by making consumers' demand for the product in question more responsive to price changes (in technical language, by making the demand curve for the product more elastic).

The practical working out of these principles constitutes the basis of the detailed policy proposals put forward later in this book. However, some of the possibilities are now fairly clear.

Without adequate knowledge of which products are, or are not, close substitutes, consumers cannot switch their purchases away from products which have risen in price. The sparse studies which have been made on the subject indicate that over a wide range of expenditure consumers' knowledge is seriously deficient (see quotation at the head of this chapter). Increasing consumer information is therefore probably the most important single step which can be taken to offset price increases. Equally important are measures for making this information more accessible to consumers and of increasing its impact.

In addition to providing consumer information, there are a variety of institutional changes which could be made to enable consumers to switch their purchases away from products which have risen in price, the precise form which these take varying from product to product. In the energy and heating field, for example, it should be obligatory for as many houses as possible (and all new houses) to be connected both for gas and electricity. The Electricity Boards have been providing substantial concessions for new houses which are "all-electric"; this is an example of a discriminatory price policy which should be made illegal. A combined gas and electricity cooker has been produced, but has not so far had much commercial success.

Low-cost alternatives could in many cases be devised by adapting existing products, and new ones could probably be produced if scientific research were consciously directed to that end. Advertising and packaging, despite their undoubted economic advantages, may result in low-cost alternatives disappearing from the market, as seems to have happened with biscuits, and nearly happened with bulk liquid detergent. It would be reasonable in such cases for consumer organizations to help the sales of low-cost products by publicity. This does not mean, of course, that such considerations should influence the purely objective work of comparative testing, or the value of the latter would be destroyed.

Intensifying competition, by measures directed against monopolies and restrictive practices, is a familiar means of increasing supply at a given price. So is productivity improvement. These subjects have given rise to a vast literature, and for that reason are not dealt with in much detail here. (A discussion of the conceptual, as distinct from the policy, aspects of monopoly is, however, a necessary preliminary to a clarification of micro-economic policies against price increases.) In recent years the possibilities of tariff-cutting, perhaps unilateral, have become more widely appreciated as a means of countering price increases, and it has been tried on a limited scale— *e.g.*, in France in 1961 and 1963, and in Spain in 1964. Tariff-cutting, and the organization of scientific research to reduce the costs of products which have risen in price, or of competing products, or the production of new competing products, constitute methods of shifting the supply curve to the right so that at any given price a larger quantity is supplied.

An increase in *quality* at a given price is equivalent from the consumers' point of view to a price reduction. Here again the main requirement is probably consumer information, without which the consumer has little basis for judging quality. Other measures could be taken to add to the life of consumer durables without increasing their cost.

Such measures as these can be accommodated within the general framework of supply and demand analysis and competition theory set out in the textbooks. They may, alternatively, be said to amount to a modification in favour of the consumer of the "rules of the game" (a rather baffling phrase much favoured by some—mainly Cambridge—economists which seems to be broadly translatable as the legal, sociological, and political framework of the price mechanism). Looked at another way, in terms of one of the major theoretical innovations in recent economic thought, they are ways in which consumers' "countervailing power" can be increased. But while an elementary grasp of the theoretical framework is essential for stating the issues to be solved and for organizing our ideas, it does not absolve us from the need to look at the facts before specific policy proposals are made, and a good deal of the latter part of this book is factual and practical rather than theoretical.

Before examining some policy possibilities in detail, it is useful to analyse more closely the power of producers and its limitations, both economic (monopoly) and producers' power in its political manifestations (pressure groups). In the outcome, the next two chapters turn out to be something of a detour, but it is at least as important to avoid misguided policies aimed at helping consumers as it is to put forward positive proposals.

CHAPTER

4

Monopoly

Monopoly growing up on the basis of free competition, and precisely out of free competition, is the transition from the capitalist to a higher social economic order.

V. I. LENIN[1]

1. *Concentration and competition*

In broad and general terms, then, the price mechanism and competition tend to ensure that the consumer gets what he wants. Whether and to what extent the position of the consumer can be improved forms the subject of the second part of this book. However, it is first necessary to investigate in some detail the major factor which has been assumed to prevent the price mechanism working to the consumer's benefit, the problem of monopoly.

If monopoly is taken as the reverse of free competition it is of course true that the strength of consumers varies inversely with the degree of monopoly, and it might be concluded that all that is necessary is to enforce and strengthen anti-monopoly legislation. In fact, the position is much more complex, and monopoly may not deserve the prominence traditionally given it in economics. Not least of the problems with which anti-monopoly legislators are faced is that of definition.

It is probably easier to start by attempting to define competition than by attempting to define monopoly. In the everyday sense, and in economic theory until about 1930, "competition" was taken to mean the existence of several firms selling the same product. Early in the 1930's, theories of imperfect or monopolistic competition were developed independently by Joan Robinson in Britain and Professor E. H. Chamberlin in the U.S.A. These theories demonstrated the stringent conditions needed for "pure" or "perfect" competition, including not only a large number of competing firms and

[1] *Imperialism* (Martin Lawrence, London, 1933), p. 111.

freedom of entry to the industry, but also absence of economies of scale, and perfect knowledge on the part of consumers and producers. Such conditions all together are seldom, if ever, encountered in practice. It is a small step from this to the further conclusion that the free enterprise economy could not bring the advantages which economists had previously assumed, though how far the originators of the theories of imperfect competition wished to derive this further conclusion has remained obscure. More recently, theories of "workable competition" (J. M. Clark, E. S. Mason, and others) have been evolved suggesting that the very stringent conditions of pure or perfect competition are not necessary in order to obtain the benefits of competition, and, insofar as they had policy implications, not very much attention is now paid to the prewar theories.

A more serious threat appeared for a time to be posed by the historical trend to larger firms and greater industrial concentration. From data on the percentage of output (or employment, or financial assets) controlled by one (or two or three) firms in certain industries, it was concluded that in many sectors of the economy monopoly was becoming more prevalent. This simplified (if not simple-minded) approach to the problem is also falling into disuse, with good reason.

In the first place, the interpretation of the statistics themselves is the subject of a good deal of technical dispute. However, it is hardly essential to enter into these disputes, as the conclusions can be criticized on more fundamental grounds. As Professor Galbraith has pointed out, it seems probable that many of the industries containing very large firms, such as oil refining, detergents, chemicals, and motor cars, are also the most competitive. (There is, unfortunately, no way of measuring the intensity of competition, so the basis for this proposition must rest mainly on common observation. The form which competition takes—whether price cutting, advertising or some other—is discussed later in this chapter.) Conversely, many industries with a large number of producing units are, or have been, rather stagnant. The textile industry was in this category until the coming of synthetic fibres, an offshoot of the chemical industry (and also until the development of cheap sources of supply in underdeveloped countries). The invasion of retailing and of some branches of farming by larger units has undoubtedly brought lower prices, though in the latter case there is scope for considerable doubt as to whether the mass-produced products (broiler eggs and poultry, etc.)

are comparable in quality with those of small units. The building industry is one of the most atomistic industries—it has the lowest statistical degree of concentration of any major industry—and has the reputation of being one of the least efficient, though it ought not to be inferred that the size of firms in the industry is a cause of its backwardness.

The mere fact that an industry has a large number of independent firms is no guarantee either of effective competition or of efficiency unless there are differences in efficiency between firms, and unless the more efficient try to increase their share of the market. A large number of firms with an equal but low degree of efficiency may result in a position of "stable equilibrium" but not much benefit to the consumer.

For several other reasons the "statistical concentration" approach to monopoly is inadequate.

(1) If one firm is substantially more efficient than all the others in an industry, it will expand and secure a major share of the market through the normal forces of competition. Any attempt to prevent it from so doing would be a restrictive practice and would bolster the inefficient. In such a situation the producers whose share of the market is being reduced (and who are thus sooner or later likely to deserve the epithet "small") may allege that the expanding firm or firms are using "unfair" competition. There may be a case for *ad hoc* investigation of such charges, but there is no case for arbitrary limitation of the share of the market held by one producer.

(2) Statistical measures of concentration derive their importance from the fact that there is believed to be a close connection between a firm's share of the market and its power to raise its prices. However, a firm which has only, say, 2 per cent of the market may have a dominating effect on prices if it is able to produce at a lower cost and undersell the larger firms (though if it can do this, its share of the market would normally grow). Even more important, potential competition may be as effective as actual competition. Unless he can keep out new competitors, a monopolist is severely limited in his power to keep up prices and profits. (This question is discussed below, "barriers to free entry".)

(3) Statistical measures of concentration frequently pay no regard to the size of the relevant market. In some cases, especially retailing and the service industries generally, the relevant market is a local one; in other cases it may be regional or international rather than

national. Statistics, on the other hand, are almost always on a national basis. This point has considerable importance in connection with, for example, controversies about resale price maintenance and the growth of large units in retailing. (It was often argued that r.p.m. helped to keep small shops in being and so benefited the consumer by preserving him from the large retailers. These latter, it was argued, would use price cutting to drive out small retailers and would then raise their prices. If this happened, however, there is no reason why small retailers should not re-enter the market—especially as the "natural" barriers to entry and exit from the retailing trades are very slight.) A shop on a particular site has an unavoidable element of natural monopoly, limited only by the closeness of other shops and the consumer's willingness and ability to travel. It follows that the growth of large enterprises in retailing is of little relevance to the question of monopoly in retailing. In fact, as mentioned, there is little doubt that the competitiveness of the retail market has increased because of the entry of large organizations; in addition, higher incomes and better travel facilities have enabled shoppers to travel farther.

(4) Tariffs are very relevant in assessing the size of the market. A manufacturer who has 70 per cent of the British market would obviously have a much smaller percentage of the enlarged market if Britain joined the European Common Market. (The same result could equally well, or better, be achieved by a world-wide or Atlantic-wide reduction of tariffs.)

(5) Concentration ratios are usually worked out on the basis of Census of Production definitions of industries, which may or may not correlate with the economic definitions. From the consumer's point of view the products of widely different industries—e.g., butter and margarine; refrigerators and frozen foods; washing machines and laundries; public houses, cinemas, and television manufacturing —are in close competition. Ultimately, of course, all goods marketed are in competition with all others, so that the appearance of any (genuinely) new product intensifies the total degree of competition. This means that:

(6) Innovation is probably the most important single limitation of the usefulness of statistical concentration ratios to indicate monopoly power. Among recent well-known examples are the impact of air travel on land and sea transport; of synthetic detergents on traditional washing materials; of plastic goods on consumer goods made of metal, wood, china, leather, and other traditional raw materials;

of television on newspaper circulation, on other forms of entertainment, and on the evening use of public transport.

(7) In many cases, the monopolists are threatened not by other firms in the same industry but by large diversified firms outside. This means that, whether actual or potential competition is under consideration, industry boundaries and the percentage of an industry's production held by one firm can be irrelevant or misleading.

To sum up, it can be said that rather than focusing attention on industrial concentration, and the extent to which it could be reduced without adversely affecting economies of scale, the central question which needs examination in a discussion of monopoly is the question of barriers to freedom of entry, and the subsidiary question of how far these are "artificial" or, on the other hand, inescapable.

2. *Barriers to free entry*

We may take as a starting-point the observation, generally agreed by textbook writers, that if above-normal profits are being earned in any industry new firms will tend to enter the industry unless there are obstacles which prevent them from doing so. This proposition is in one sense circular and merely a definition of "normal profit" (which concept, as pointed out by Adam Smith,[2] is almost entirely subjective). Nevertheless the statement has practical relevance. If high profits persist in any industry for a considerable period of time it will probably be useful to examine the conditions of entry into the industry. It must be noted that the converse does not hold true—the *absence* of high profits is not an indication that conditions of entry, or any other aspect of the monopoly problem, should *not* be examined, since many (and perhaps most) forms of monopolistic "exploitation" are likely to take the form of high costs rather than high profits.

Barriers to free entry may be divided in principle into those inherent in the productive process, and those which are capable of being reduced. The most important of the first kind are those which exist when economies of scale are so important that a firm has to supply a substantial part of the industry's output in order to attain the optimum size of plant or firm (the latter must be included as economies of scale may be managerial, marketing or financial as

---

[2] He referred to businessmen "who speak of a good, moderate, reasonable profit; by which terms, I apprehend, they mean no more than a common or usual profit." (*Wealth of Nations*, Ch. IX "Of the Profits of Stock").

well as technical), or those where the capital requirements of establishing a new plant or firm are very large in absolute terms. If a new firm entered such an industry at a time when existing firms were at or near the optimum size the result would be either excess capacity and higher costs, or competition leading to the elimination of one or more firms (though this kind of situation can arise only when the price-elasticity of demand for the product is not high—*i.e.*, "cutthroat" price competition does not lead to expansion of the market; or, if competition takes the form of advertising, this does not lead to expansion of the market). Where these conditions are to be found, oligopoly (a small number of firms) obviously has to be accepted—whatever its merits or drawbacks in principle.

Other obstacles to free entry, which might be mitigated to some degree, are patents, control of raw materials, monopoly of expert management or skilled labour, backward or forward integration leading to monopolization of suppliers or sales outlets, product differentiation, and advertising. Patents are a legal device and if it were desired to amend the law so as to stimulate competition no insuperable obstacles should arise. Control of raw materials is of decreasing importance. Vertical integration is normally expensive; some economists hold that the tendency of modern business is in the opposite direction, towards vertical disintegration, and it is difficult to think of many cases where control of, for example, suppliers of components or retail outlets has provided a lasting monopoly. (The former would in any case be very difficult so long as there are free imports; the latter would have to be on a very large scale to produce an effective monopoly in every retail district.) Monopolies based on control of management or labour skills can, or at least should, be relatively easy to overcome with efficient training methods.

The *a priori* conclusion that in general economies arising from economies of scale, and from product differentiation and/or advertising, are likely to be the only obstacles of long-run major significance, is supported by the conclusions of the only serious attempt to study barriers to free entry quantitatively over a wide range of industries, J. S. Bain's book, *Barriers to New Competition*.[3] Bain says:

Perhaps the most surprising finding of our study—if previous casual comment on barriers to entry is taken as the standard—is

[3] Harvard University Press, 1956. p. 216.

that the most important barrier to entry discovered by detailed study is probably product differentiation. That is, the advantage to established sellers accruing from buyer preferences for their products as opposed to potential-entrant[s'] products is on the average larger and more frequent in occurrence at large values than any other barrier to entry. This is in any event apparently true of our sample of 20 industries,[5] and the writer is by now prepared to guess that it is true in general. . . . In some cases—e.g., cigarettes, liquor and quality fountain-pens—product differentiation almost alone is responsible for very high aggregate existing entry barriers. In others—automobiles, tractors, typewriters—it combines with very important economies of scale in production to produce extremely high barriers.

This verdict puts in quite a new perspective the old, and necessarily somewhat inconclusive, argument about whether product differentiation as it exists at present simply reflects the consumer's desire for variety or whether it is carried on to a "wasteful" extent (presumably, to an extent which makes it difficult for firms to achieve economies of large-scale production). It is fairly clear that a wide range of choice for consumers involves the marketing of as wide a range of products as is compatible with the existence of near-optimum-sized firms. It is further clear that not only physical and technically verifiable differences between products are desirable. In many industries, especially where there is no reason to believe that brand-limitation would bring economies of production and lower prices, a wide range of choice must be regarded as an end in itself. Wartime experience with single "national" brands of chocolate or cigarettes showed that many consumers were prepared to pay more in order to get a non-standardized brand.

But product differentiation sustained by continuous heavy advertising presents a more vulnerable target for its critics. (The word "continuous" must be stressed. There is general agreement that heavy advertising is necessary to introduce new products and new brands.) Bain suggests "measures to restrict advertising expenditures, either absolutely or by taxation" and suggests that "measures such as comprehensive grade labelling or its equivalent, plus perhaps wide public dissemination of product information, would also

<hr>

4 Insertion by present author.
5 The industries studies by Bain were automobiles, canned goods, cement, cigarettes, copper, farm machinery, flour, fountain-pens, gypsum products, liquor, meat packing, metal containers, petroleum refining, rayon, shoes, soap, steel, tyres and tubes, tractors, and typewriters.

be salutary, especially if they proceeded far enough to dissipate the advantages of nationwide sales promotion."[6]

The three cases where Bain found product differentiation alone to be a very serious barrier to free entry—cigarettes, liquor, and "quality" fountain-pens—are peculiar in different ways. Both in Britain and the U.S.A., cigarettes and liquor are subject to very high taxation. In consequence, price cuts by manufacturers have little effect on retail prices, and competition tends to take the form mainly of advertising. The peculiarity about "quality" fountain-pens is that, as several market research surveys have shown, they are bought mainly as gifts, and as a consequence within certain price ranges demand varies directly with price, and increases if the price is raised, rather than vice versa as with the great majority of consumer goods.

In assessing the importance of advertising and product differentiation as barriers to freedom of entry, it is important to look at the entire market situation. Heavy advertising by one or more firms in an industry in which there are a large number of firms can hardly in itself be said to lead to a reduction of competition. The prime importance of innovation in countering monopoly has been noted already; in many consumer-goods industries heavy advertising will be necessary, initially at least, to overcome consumer resistance to new products. One recent example is detergents, though here heavy advertising persisted long after it was necessary for the purpose of promoting a new product.[7] In the professions, blanket restrictions on advertising may operate to restrict the scope for newcomers at the

---

[6] Bain goes on (*op. cit.*, p. 217): "The writer does not suggest that any or all of these measures is politically feasible, but they seem to embody the only apparent means of attack on excessive product-differentiation barriers to entry." This comment is rather difficult to follow, except perhaps in the political context of the U.S.A. In Britain measures to limit advertising have been widely discussed, and following the report of the Monopolies Commission on detergents in August 1966 were put into effect as regards the major producers; while the need for much wider consumer information seems to be almost universally agreed.

[7] The Report of the Monopolies Commission on "Synthetic Detergents" (August 1966) concluded (para. 121) with regard to the two major companies in the U.K. market, Unilever and Proctor and Gamble: "The return on capital earned by both of these on household detergents is high, and in one case it is very high. This situation arises because the competition between them is concentrated in the field of advertising and promotion. This not only results in wasteful expenditure but also deters potential competitors, who might, otherwise, provide a safeguard against excessive profits."

expense of established firms, and heavier advertising in such a situation would promote competitiveness, not monopoly.[8] The need for case-by-case study of market situations cannot be avoided.

It seems clear, however, that there *are* cases—concentrated industries, advertising in the hands of large established firms, and advertising not essential to promote innovation or for other purposes—in which product differentiation sustained by heavy advertising constitutes a serious barrier to the entry of new firms. In such cases consumer information is needed, but is unlikely to be sufficient. Limitation of the volume of advertising may also be desirable.

3. *Advertising and non-price competition*

There is evidence that product differentiation, supported by heavy advertising, constitutes one of the most important barriers to freedom of entry, especially in the consumer-goods field. But advertising cannot be judged solely by its effects on freedom of entry and we must here review briefly the economic effects of advertising.

Perhaps inevitably, advertising tends to attract an excessive amount of attention. Both critics of advertising and its supporters (including its practitioners) often attribute to it an unwarranted degree of influence. In fact, progress towards measuring the effectiveness of advertising has been very slow, and while some of the problems involved are soluble with improved techniques, others are likely to be insoluble in principle. Frequently it is impossible to attribute particular changes in a manufacturer's sales to changes in his advertising expenditure, as so many other factors (consumers' tastes and incomes, the behaviour of his competitors) are changing at the same time. Advertising which is highly successful in attracting the attention of the reader (or viewer or listener) may be less successful in selling the product; such appears to have been the case with the admirable Guinness posters. While the successful advertising campaigns remain (and are kept) in the public eye, the numerous

---

[8] See Professor D. S. Lees, *Economic Consequences of the Professions*, (Institute of Economic Affairs, 1966). There is of course a case for very much more stringent safeguards against *misleading* advertising where the professions are concerned than is the case with goods and services. If professional advertising were allowed it would presumably be limited to an announcement of address, services carried out, and suchlike. The need for such advertising is particularly evident in the case of architects. Their efficiency suffers from fluctuations in the work-load of individual offices, which advertising could help to stabilize. (See F. Knox and J. Hennessy, *Restrictive Practices in the Building Industry*, Institute of Economic Affairs, 1966).

unsuccessful ones—*e.g.,* to persuade men to wear hats, or to make soup a breakfast food—tend to be forgotten. When we come to the wider social, as distinct from economic, effects of advertising there is even less evidence on which to base dogmatic opinions. Certainly there does not seem to be much to be said for the school of thought which attributes almost all social ills, from dental decay to sexual delinquency, to advertising.[9]

Apart from the all-pervasive uncertainty about its effects, the prime factor which tends to be overlooked in most discussions of advertising is that the relevant distinction to be drawn is between price and non-price competition, not between advertising and other forms of competition. Non-price competition includes quality, design, availability, after-sales service, and sales promotion. Where resale price maintenance or recommended prices exist it also includes the very important factor of margins offered to retailers by manufacturers. "Sales promotion" includes, besides advertising proper, such methods as gift coupons (given by manufacturers or retailers), trading stamps, the numerous kinds of consumer competitions, free gifts (plastic flowers given with detergents, toys with breakfast cereals, ballpoint pens or toilet soap given with toothpaste, nylon stockings and dusters given with a variety of products), and so on, besides taking on such indirect manifestations as car rallies sponsored by car manufacturers, beauty queen competitions, etc. Where retailers are concerned, non-price competition includes efficiency of service, stock layout, credit and delivery terms, advertising, and location (though manufacturers' prestige offices in central locations may also be regarded as a form of advertising).

While in general it may be said that any form of competition is better than none, some of these varieties are obviously more beneficial to the consumer than others; in particular, price competition is usually better than non-price except where the non-price is such as to be directly translatable into its price equivalent, as with location and delivery. However, once we recognize the multifarious forms which competition can take, and that in devising his marketing strategy the producer will regard them as to some extent substitutable for each other, proposals for restricting one form of

---

[9] On the other hand it seems fair to attribute to petrol advertising some of the responsibility for road accidents, and to cigarette advertising some of the resulting mortality. Patent medicine advertising to the general public presents special problems, which in the author's view could not be dealt with short of complete prohibition.

competition, such as advertising, are seen in general to be impracticable. (Thus, for example, limitation of cigarette advertising in Britain in 1966 led to a revival of gift coupons.)

If government controls were to be extended in an attempt to reduce *all* forms of non-price competition, or at least all forms except those such as quality improvement which clearly benefit the consumer, problems of supervising the activities and products of individual firms would arise similar to those arising from price control, and the administrative effort might be substantial.

If we disregard any general action limiting advertising and sales promotion we are left with two major questions of explanation and of policy. First, why is it that in many oligopolistic consumer-goods industries competition generally takes the form of advertising rather than price competition? Secondly, can non-price competition lead in the long run to increases in costs, and in prices to the consumer? Neither economic theory nor empirical study can as yet provide definitive answers to these questions, but some pointers are available.

Taking the second question first, competition in sales promotion is often said to be analogous to an arms race in which each participant would be better off if it were stopped, but in which each must go on increasing his expenditure while others do so. In the short run, such kinds of situation obviously exist. But if each producer is increasing his selling expenditure, and if in consequence prices are being raised, there will come a point when one or more producers will find it in their interest to desist and cut prices. Clearly the point at which this happens depends mainly on the price-consciousness of consumers, which in turn depends partly on the information available to consumers. Once it is appreciated that from the producer's point of view the different forms of competition are alternatives, the question of whether competition can lead to higher costs—the "wastes of competition"—becomes easier to answer. The arms race analogy is not in fact a good one, for producers have an alternative to non-price competition in price cutting.

The most useful measure for strengthening price competition is to increase the price consciousness of consumers. How far this can be done, and at what cost, it is not possible to say until more experience is available. The existing degree of price consciousness and means of increasing it is a subject urgently in need of basic and applied research.[10] (Some possibilities for reducing the cost, both to individual consumers and in real economic terms, of consumer information are discussed in Chapter 7.)

Why does oligopolistic competition frequently take the form of advertising rather than price cutting?

Manufacturers in oligopolistic industries may realize, consciously or not, that heavy advertising may be a deterrent to new entrants more than low prices. They may believe, rightly or wrongly, that consumers respond more to advertising in terms of increased consumption than they would to price reductions. However, if the latter is the explanation, it is clear that the form competition takes will depend as much on the price elasticity of demand for the product as on the number of producers in the industry. Thus we would expect, quite irrespective of the number of firms in the industry, that there would be heavier advertising in industries such as soap, cigarettes, and chocolate, where the unit price of the product is small, than in industries such as cars and other consumer durables where the product is fairly expensive and consumers will probably devote some thought to weighing the merits of alternative brands before buying.

But the question to some extent prejudges the issue, and is of the "Have you stopped beating your wife?" form. While it is true that many oligopolistic consumer-goods industries are characterized by heavy advertising,[11] some—e.g., matches, sugar-refining, motorcycles, photographic films, typewriters—are not; one of the deciding factors seems to be greater consumer knowledge in most of these cases. Also, even industries such as detergents, cigarettes, and chocolate are subject to occasional outbreaks of price competition. In synthetic detergents, the introduction of new kinds of detergent by Procter and Gamble early in the 1950's was accompanied by very heavy advertising, which forced Unilever to advertise in self-defence. In 1955 Unilever adopted a policy of reduction both in prices and

[10] The only factual investigation known to the author is that reported in *Economica*, February 1966, "Price as an indicator of quality", by A. Gabor and C. W. J. Granger.

[11] The assumption that this is so is stated in many textbooks—for example, R. Dorfman, *The Price System* (Prentice-Hall Inc., 1964): "We have already remarked the firm determination with which oligopolists eschew the use of prices in maintaining and advancing their market positions. In lieu of this instrument, oligopolists rely on two others: competition through advertising and merchandising efforts, and competition through style changes and product improvement."

advertising, and a price war was initiated which lasted until 1957. At the latter date a further round of product innovation began, accompanied by further advertising.[12] Later, liquid detergents for washing-up were introduced, some produced by firms other than the two main protagonists, and the degree of oligopoly was reduced. Finally, if account is taken of concealed price reductions through quality and size improvements, free gifts and "3d off" offers, etc., the assumption that in oligopolistic industries competition takes the form mainly of advertising is still further undermined.

4. *"Administered prices"*

An interesting concept which has emerged from recent discussion of inflation is that of "administered prices". Some economists hold that where there are administered prices, as with large monopolistic firms or trade unions, there is scope for direct government intervention to prevent prices rising by persuasion or control of individual firms.

The idea had its origin in a U.S. Senate document of 1935 called "Industrial prices and their relative inflexibility", by Gardiner C. Means, then economic adviser to the U.S. Department of Agriculture. It was developed in a book by G. C. Means and Caroline Ware published the following year, *The Modern Economy in Action*.[13] Initially, the concept of administered prices was designed to show that farmers were at a disadvantage in an industrial economy, as the prices of their purchases (both in their capacity as consumers, and as producers—fertilizers, farm requisites, etc.) were controlled by the suppliers of these products, while the prices at which they sold their farm produce were at the mercy of the free market. In the post-war inflation era it has received a wider application, and has been used to explain the fact that the cost of living in most countries has continued to rise despite government measures to limit total demand by the traditional weapons of monetary policy and budget surpluses.

More specifically, it is intended to explain the fact that in many industries, especially those dominated by a few large firms, prices have continued to rise—or at least have not been reduced—even when demand for the product was falling and there was unemployment and excess capacity in the industry.

[12] Monopolies Commission report on Synthetic Detergents, paras. 18 and 19.
[13] Harcourt, Brace & Co., New York, 1936.

Steel prices continued to rise in face of a relatively low demand level for steel and much unemployment in the industry. . . . In a free market, "if supply exceeded demand, the price would fall until supply and demand were in balance. . . . We do not have such a market system in an economy dominated by large corporations. The decision to raise steel prices in the summer of 1958 did not reflect the automatic forces of the market place. It was an administrative decision and the resulting prices were administered prices.[14]

Between 1957 and 1963 the U.S. Senate Sub-Committee on Anti-Trust and Monopoly, under the chairmanship of the late Senator Kefauver, held hearings on administered prices in the steel, automobile, tyre, drug, and baking industries. It was clear, however, by the end of the hearings that the Committee was interpreting the idea of administered prices so broadly as to make it almost meaningless. Any criticism which could be made of these industries was incorporated under the umbrella. When considering the drug industry the Committee concerned itself with the volume and content of advertising; in the automobile industry with the effect of model changes on prices; in the steel industry, it was worried that the high prices might lead to a further reduction in employment in the industry; while in the baking industry its main concern was the growth of large units, possibly due to unfair competition, and the decline in the number of small firms. The criticisms made of the industries concerned were doubtless valid, but it would have clarified matters if the hearings had been recognized simply as *ad hoc* investigations of the various industries. Excepting the point about prices and employment in the steel industry, there is no valid reason why the matters mentioned above should have been discussed under "administered prices".[15]

As well as covering a multitude of sins, the concept suffers from fundamental ambiguities. In many industries it is true that prices remain steady in spite of a fall in demand; similarly, in a period of shortage, a manufacturer may prefer to hold prices steady and use informal rationing to balance supply and demand. This occurred, for example, in the car industry in Britain after the Second World War, when an acute shortage was reflected in long waiting-lists. But, as a simple supply-and-demand diagram may be used to demonstrate, if

[14] Gardiner C. Means, *Pricing Power and the Public Interest* (Harper and Bros., New York, 1962), p. 10.
[15] The essence of the Kefauver hearings is included in E. Kefauver, *In a Few Hands—Monopoly Power in America* (Penguin Books, 1966).

E

the price of a product is held steady despite a shift to the left of the demand curve (*i.e.*, a fall in demand) production and employment will be lower after the new equilibrium is reached than if the price had in fact been allowed to fall.

In agriculture, when demand falls the effect is felt on price rather than on production and employment (at least in the absence of outside intervention). Hence *cyclical* unemployment of the kind found in industry is almost unknown in agriculture, while there are alarmingly wide swings in prices. But it is by no means certain that producers as a whole are worse off under the "agricultural" as opposed to the "industrial" type of situation in periods of a *temporary* fall in demand. (We are ignoring here the question of long-term changes in the terms of trade between industry and agriculture.) In neither case is it clear that producers can stabilize their incomes by stabilizing prices.

To explain the different patterns of behaviour in industry and agriculture, there are a number of alternatives to the "administered prices" concept. The textbook explanations of monopoly and competition show that the monopolistic firm has much more discretion over the price which it charges. The monopolist producer faces a sloping demand curve, while under perfect competition the demand curve for the individual firm's product is a horizontal straight line. But the monopolist's demand curve may be inelastic only in the short run; in the longer term its demand may become much more elastic as competing industries invent substitutes—as the U.S. steel industry, usually held to be the classic instance of "administered prices", has discovered.

In the context of cyclical changes, a *sufficiently severe* recession might force many producers to cut their prices, including those who held their prices during the relatively mild recessions of the post-war period. Similarly, British car manufacturers might have raised their prices during the post-war shortage but for the fact that they realized that it would only be temporary.

Whether we are concerned with (or about) the incomes of producers, or prices charged to consumers, the theory of administered prices seems to be barking up the wrong tree. The fact that in large industrial organizations prices are held steady for as long as possible may well be a result of the administrative difficulty of making price changes which has been discussed in Chapter 3 in connection with price control. The prices of consumer goods may change less frequently than those of capital goods (which are in any case fre-

quently the subject of individual negotiation) and it is certainly true
that they change less frequently than those of raw materials, whose
prices on the commodity markets fluctuate hourly. These facts are
not, however, of central or vital significance for economic policy provided there is competition at all stages of the productive process, and
adequate consumer knowledge.

One critic of the concept has written:

> The great bulk of prices are administered. They are not ob-
> served in the course of an irregular stream of bids matching
> offers; the seller (or less often the buyer) announces the price by
> a deliberate act, sometimes after a good deal of bureaucratic
> effort. But this is form, not substance; a description of how prices
> are announced tells us nothing of why they are what they are and
> not other than what they are. . . . The theory of "administered
> prices" is appealing because it provides a phrase which seems to
> explain everything. Thereby it liberates us from the need to work
> at explaining the forces of supply and demand. . . . There is a
> deeply-felt need for both kinds of freedom.[16]

The theory does nevertheless lead to one important conclusion. It
may be that political pressures on manufacturers not to raise prices,
of the kind used since 1960 in several countries, and perhaps even
legal control of prices, have some chance of success when there is
a state of recession in the economy as a whole or in particular industries. If this kind of pressure is successful the impact of a fall in
demand will be felt more on prices, and less on production and
employment, than would otherwise be the case. Whether it can be
successful over a succession of periods of recession is a matter of
political and historical judgment, and there is a danger that governments will attribute to their "prices and incomes policies" results
which are mainly due to holding down demand.

5. Conclusion

The tenor of this chapter has been largely negative. We have stressed
the difficulties in defining monopoly, we have suggested that statistical concentration ratios tend to exaggerate the power over prices of
individual firms, and we have rejected the idea that there is a
distinct class of "administered prices" which needs special attention.
We have argued that advertising does not deserve the attention

[16] M. A. Adleman, "Steel, administered prices and inflation", *Quarterly
Journal of Economics*, February 1961, pp. 18–19.

accorded it by some of its critics, and that there would be a case for restricting it only if an oligopolistic firm were relying mainly on advertising to keep out new competition. We have argued that the questions requiring factual investigation are not the number of firms in an industry or the frequency with which prices are changed, but obstacles to free entry and to the effectiveness of price competition. For both these latter questions consumer information is of considerable, and perhaps decisive, importance.

If a firm acquires a dominant position by *mergers* rather than by "natural" expansion of sales at the expense of other firms, there is certainly a case for close attention to the subsequent course of events, particularly the subsequent course of prices. At present in Britain the Board of Trade, under the Monopolies and Mergers Act of 1965, is empowered to examine proposed mergers and to prohibit them if it thinks they would be harmful. However, it might be more useful if powers existed to scrutinize, perhaps continuously, the course of events *following* a merger. Another way of increasing competition would be to require profit figures to be published in greater detail, so that new firms would be more easily attracted into areas where large profits are being made. In the car industry one of the "unintentional" barriers to free entry is after-sales service, and there might be a case for enforcing on garages an obligation to service any make of car, if this can be done without reducing the efficiency of the service. In traditional anti-monopoly legislation there is probably scope for tightening legislation against restrictive practices, especially in connection with "information agreements"; though one of the major restrictive practices on the management side, the filling of managerial posts by family connections or nepotism, is one which it would be difficult to deal with by legislation. But when all these lines of action have been explored it may well turn out that the most important single measure to increase the effectiveness of competition is consumer information.

Thus, the topic which is usually referred to in footnotes and asides in economics textbooks comes, Cinderella-fashion, to take the centre of the stage, and the *personae* of Monopoly and Oligopoly, to which so much attention has been devoted in economics, come to play, if not a shadow role, at least a fairly minor one.

CHAPTER

5

Pressure Groups and Economic Interest

> The interest of the dealers, however, in any particular branch
> of trade or manufacture, is always in some respects different
> from, and even opposite to, that of the public.
>
> ADAM SMITH[1]

1. *The phenomenon and its setting*

A pressure group may be defined as a body representing an economic interest and trying to exercise influence on elected representatives, the executive, political parties, and public opinion. Some authorities object to the term "pressure group" on the grounds that most of the time such organizations are merely concerned with putting their case, not with threatening; Professor Finer prefers the term "the Lobby".[2] Also, many pressure groups do not primarily represent economic interests. In Britain the latter include the Lord's Day Observance Society, the Union for the Abolition of Vivisection, the Noise Abatement Society, Church organizations, and so on. Further difficulties of definition now emerge: the trade unions would undoubtedly claim to have ideological aims in addition to the aim of advancing the interests of their members, and actions even by purely ideological bodies may have economic implications. However, for present purposes the rough definition given above is adequate.

Outside the U.S.A., where studies of pressure groups appeared in the late 1920's, the subject has only recently been studied systematically. The first two academic studies of pressure groups published in Britain did not appear until 1958,[3] although the Trades Union

---

[1] Book I, Chapter XI, "Of the rent of the land."

[2] S. E. Finer, *Anonymous Empire* (Pall Mall Press, London, 1958), p. 3.

[3] S. E. Finer (*op. cit.*,) and J. D. Stewart, *British Pressure Groups* (Oxford University Press, 1958).

Congress dates from 1868, the National Farmers' Union from 1908, and the Federation of British Industries (now the Confederation of British Industry) from 1917. The last-named was established "to enable industry to speak with one voice" (a favourite phrase in pressure-group circles) to the government on problems of post-war reconstruction and is now the recognized spokesman for business. Since the Second World War these and other organized interests have come to play an increasingly important role. The T.U.C. has become, in the phrase of Sir Winston Churchill, a "fourth estate of the realm" and the National Farmers' Union gained greatly enhanced status with the annual price-review procedure embodied in the Agriculture Act of 1947.

To a considerable degree, the formalization of pressure groups is a response to increased government intervention in the economy. It is significant that during the Second World War the government actually took the initiative in some cases in promoting representative organizations, in industries where these did not already exist, in order to have an "opposite number" with which it could negotiate. Recently, with the government (national and local) spending one-third of the national income, and accepting responsibility not only for maintaining full employment but for promoting economic growth, the scope for private representative bodies to negotiate with the government is not likely to diminish. Since the war, too, many old-established professional organizations such as the British Medical Association and the National Union of Teachers have begun to play a more active part in promoting the economic interests of their members, and under the strains of inflation trade unionism has made considerable gains in white-collar domains such as civil servants and bank employees.

There existed for long, and may still exist in extreme left-wing and right-wing quarters, a tendency to regard pressure groups as sinister and undesirable.[4] (One of the more naïve attempts to prove the political power of business listed the persons with high positions in private firms or trade associations who were co-opted into government-instituted trade supervisory bodies during the war, failing to

[4] John Strachey, Laski, and other socialist writers suggested before the war that a serious attempt by a socialist government to reduce or regulate the power of private capital would be met by sabotage, such as the engineering of a financial crisis. Such theories are hardly supported by the experience of post-war Labour governments and are effectively criticized in S. E. Finer, "The political power of private capital", *The Sociological Review* (University College of Keele), 1955–56.

recognize that their monopoly of commercial and technical know-ledge made such co-option almost inevitable.[5]) However the prevalent, and undoubtedly correct, view among political scientists is that pressure groups are a necessary, and to some extent a desirable, concomitant of the democratic process. Little more is involved here than the argument that freedom must involve freedom to combine in order to advance one's own interests, though the legal framework within which such groups act should not be left to the interests concerned to decide (as with the prohibition of restrictive business practices and of bribery).

Conflicts of economic interest exist, whether or not they are manifested in formal organizations. The outstanding aim should be that pressure groups should be open and not concealed, "open pressure politics openly conducted."[6] But it is also a truism that in pressure politics weak or unorganized groups may be neglected; among such groups have been numbered, until recently, consumers.

2. *How do pressure groups operate?*

It is sometimes suggested that in a modern democracy a decline in the economic position of any economic group may be expected to lead to economic and political action to reverse the trend, though it cannot, of course, be assumed that such action will always be successful, or there would be no relative changes in the economic status of different groups. A study of farmers' political action concludes:

> A factor of great importance in the setting off of political movements is an abrupt change for the worse in the status of one group relative to that of other groups in society. The economics of politics is by no means simply a matter of poor against rich; the rich and poor may live peaceably for decades, each accepting its status quietly. A rapid change for the worse, however, in the relative status of any group, rich or poor, is likely to precipitate political action. Depression has been closely associated with manifestations of farmers' political action.[7]

This assumption is also found in one of the major contributions

[5] A. A. Rogow and Peter Shore, *The Labour Government and British Industry* (Blackwell, Oxford, 1955).

[6] Graham Wootton, *The Politics of Influence: British Ex-servicemen, Cabinet Decisions and Cultural Change, 1917–1957* (Routledge and Kegan Paul, 1963), p. 263.

[7] Ross B. Talbot, "The changing political position of agriculture," *Journal of Farm Economics*, May 1963, p. 318.

to the economic theory of pressure groups, Professor J. K. Galbraith's theory of "countervailing power".[8] According to this theory a substantial accretion of economic power—presumably in the conditions prevailing in the United States—will tend to give rise to offsetting reactions. The economic strength of large manufacturers led to the rise of large retail chains, which use their buying power to force down prices, while the economic strength of employers gave rise to labour unions. Thus, although competition within industries may have declined, new restrictions on private power have grown up to replace them, "but they appeared not on the same side of the market but on the opposite side, not with competitors but with customers or suppliers."[9]

As a supplement to more orthodox theories of competition, "countervailing power" is now generally accepted. However, as with all comprehensive theories in social science, difficulties arise in its application. It is not clear how far it is intended to embrace political action—*i.e.*, government measures to improve the position of underprivileged sectors of the community. (If countervailing power always developed autonomously there would be no need for the government to intervene.)

Galbraith seems to intend the theory to be a guide to policy as well as a purely explanatory one:

> Without the phenomenon being fully recognized . . . state assistance to the development of countervailing power has become a major function of government—perhaps *the* major function of government. Much of the domestic legislation of the last twenty years, that of the New Deal episode in particular, only becomes comprehensible when viewed in this light.[10]

A relative decline in the economic status of a group may be a major factor in initiating political action by or on behalf of the group, but there are very many other factors in determining whether it is successful.

A naïve approach might indicate that the strength of a pressure group is a product of the (adult or electoral) population in the group multiplied by the effectiveness of the organization. However, it becomes apparent on investigation that the situation is much more complex, and in some ways the reverse is true. That the percentage

[8] *American Capitalism* (Houghton Mifflin, Boston, 1952).

[9] *American Capitalism* (Hamish Hamilton, London, 1956, 2nd edition), p. 111.

[10] *op. cit.*, p. 128.

of population is not decisive is shown by the increasing influence of agriculture in the political economy of Britain, the U.S.A., and other countries during the past twenty—or, indeed, hundred—years despite the steady fall in the numbers employed in agriculture during the period. And if numbers were the decisive factor, consumers should be the most powerful pressure group, when in fact their influence has often been slight. Consumers may in the past have scored notable victories, but many of them were probably due to the help of powerful allies. For example, the repeal of the Corn Laws in 1846 is attributed by historians to the desire of manufacturers for cheap food (in order to keep down wages and hence manufacturing costs). Electorally, it is a well-known fact that a group which holds the balance of power may be able to obtain an influence out of proportion to its numbers. Conversely, except where there is proportional representation, electors in areas where there is effective balance may find their influence reduced. A Labour Party majority in an industrial constituency may be so large that a particular pressure group, such as cotton workers and their employers in Lancashire, can exert little influence; a threat to vote Conservative would have little credibility. Similarly a Conservative majority in a rural area might be so large that a farmers' organization could not exert influence by threatening to vote Labour (though even if these hypothetical situations existed in some constituencies, nationally the position might be different).

Further evidence that influence is not directly related to numbers is the fact that old-age pensioners have not much improved their economic position relative to that of the community as a whole (though they have, of course, improved their absolute position) as their numbers have increased. One authority comments: "Older people have the lowest incomes; retirement means an abridgement of income; they have the lowest social significance since that significance is afforded by the part played in the productive process; they are inarticulate, dispersed and unorganized; but even if they were organized, their supposed 'pressure group' would be very poor in terms of pressure; of course they cannot strike."[11] But a time-lag may be at work in this instance and it is conceivable that in the future old-age pensioners may be able to improve their relative position purely by electoral means.

Another factor to be taken into account is expectations. Professor

[11] Bertrand de Jouvenal, "The future of the aged", *The Spectator*, March 13th, 1964.

Gunnar Myrdal suggests that motor-car owners constitute a powerful pressure group even in countries where car ownership is low, as most people *hope* some day to own a car. Myrdal argues for the same reason (contrary to de Jouvenal) that old people are fairly well protected, as everyone knows that he will one day come within this category. The least protected, according to Myrdal, are small groups such as "criminals and mentally-deranged or feeble-minded persons and their dependants. They are few, and they are not easily organized; and the incidence of the misfortune of becoming one of them is so small—or is in any case commonly considered to be so small— that solidarity with them among the outside community is difficult to mobilize."[12] Other groups which might be added are widows, fatherless families, and recent immigrants (women, to the extent that they have not achieved equal pay and equal opportunity, may also be regarded as underprivileged.)

Besides electoral action—the threat of voting for the other party —the main threat which a pressure group can wield is that of withholding goods or services. A business organization can raise prices by limiting supplies (within the limitations discussed in the last chapter); a labour organization can, within different but also considerable limitations, raise wages by striking. Non-producer groups such as old-age pensioners cannot, of course, use these weapons. It might appear that the power of a labour or professional group would depend mainly on its power to strike and the effectiveness of strike action, but here again the position turns out to be much more complex—partly because, as Professor Finer points out, most of the action of pressure groups is not in using or threatening sanctions but in other activities, such as influencing public opinion. (This fact is of relevance to the discussion of the prospects of a consumer strike, discussed in the next chapter.) However, the power of striking is certainly an important factor, and as far as trade unions are concerned the question: "What determines the strength of a pressure group?" turns largely on the further question: "Under what circumstances is a strike for higher wages likely to be successful?"

Generally strike action is taken only by non-professional workers, though in recent years it has also been adopted by other groups. In 1956 there was a prolonged teachers' strike in Ireland, in 1962 a farmers' strike in the mid-West of the U.S.A., in 1964 a doctors' strike in Belgium. Threats of strikes or partial strikes are more frequent—*e.g.*, the doctors in Britain threatened to withdraw from the

[12] *Beyond the Welfare State* (Duckworth, London, 1960), pp. 80–81.

National Health Service in 1948 unless pay was increased, and teachers have refused to supervise school meals or to do clerical work. The reluctance of professional groups to use the strike weapon is attributable to professional ethics, the fact that individual advancement is the normal method of progress (in contrast to manual workers, who must act collectively in order to get any increase in wages), and also perhaps to the knowledge that a substantial number of their members would "blackleg". It is not clear that the reluctance of professions to use the strike weapon has led to a deterioration of their relative economic status (if the latter has occurred, it is probably mainly due to the progressiveness of the income tax system).

3. *The monopoly power of trade unions*

The economist's answer to the question "When is a strike for higher wages likely to be successful?" is that it depends on the one hand on the elasticity of substitution between labour and capital, (*i.e.*, the extent to which employers in the industry concerned can substitute capital for labour if the price of the latter rises relatively to that of the former); and on the other hand on the elasticity of demand for the final product of the firm or industry. This goes some way, but not the whole way, to an explanation. There are two complicating factors: supply and demand for labour will be influenced by institutional factors; and conclusions reached at the micro-economic level, assuming other things to remain equal, may be inapplicable if wages in many industries are rising simultaneously.

Professional bodies and trade unions often try to limit the supply of labour in their respective occupations. Periods of training in themselves constitute an important obstacle to increasing the supply of labour, though how far this is a removable obstacle can be determined only after empirical investigation in any particular case. In many cases the demand for labour is largely "political". The demand for local government employees and civil servants, doctors, teachers and university employees is decided not by market forces but by how many the government decides are needed. The volume of employment in other occupations such as farming, aircraft manufacture, and arms production is also determined wholly or partly by government decision.

However, where the demand for labour is not primarily determined by the government, the "supply and demand" explanation of wage levels in particular industries contains an indispensable element of truth. Relative wages have never been shown to be closely related to the "degree of unionization" or any other measure of union power. A U.S. study concluded that "There does not appear to be any significant correlation between union strength and/or changes in union strength on the one hand and changes in labour's relative income share within the manufacturing industries studied."[13] The conclusion derives some support from casual observation, such as the fact that typists, who have no trade union, have gained wage increases greater than the national average as demand has expanded.

There are, however, a number of distinctions to be made. There are three possible subjects for investigation: whether trade unions influence the *relative share* of the product in the industries in which they operate; whether they influence *real wages*; and whether they influence *money wages*. Approaching the subject from the standpoint of monopoly analysis, the first two questions are the important ones. But for understanding the causes of and remedies for inflation, money wages is the central issue. Trade unions may have little or no influence on the long-term share of the national product, or the share of labour in product of particular industries, or on real wages, and still be a major factor in the inflationary spiral. Unions may obtain increases in money wages, the extent of the increase depending on the degree of union power, and the wage increases may be cancelled out by rises in prices. This is probably the most widely-accepted explanation of inflation among non-economists. A variety of subsidiary factors could be added to this "model": for example, once strongly unionized trades had obtained a wage increase, the factor of "comparability", if this is widely accepted as a ground for wage increases, might lead to a diffusion of similar wage increases throughout the economy.

In fact, the most thorough study yet made of the subject indicates that, as regards increases in *money wages*, the strength of trade unions *is* a major factor. Professor A. G. Hines, taking the *rate of change* of the percentage of the labour force unionized as his index of trade-union power, concludes that this index of trade-union pushfulness "makes a statistically significant contribution to the explanation of the total variation in wage rates. Indeed, in the inter-war and post-war years, it is the most powerful of all explanatory variables."[14] (Although Professor Hines does not raise the question,

---

[13] N. J. Simler, *The impact of unionism on wage-income ratios in the manufacturing sector of the economy* (University of Minnesota Press, 1961), p. 175.
[14] A. G. Hines, "Trade unions and wage inflation in the U.K., 1893–1961", *Review of Economic Studies*, 1964, pp. 221–252.

this intriguing conclusion raises the further possibility that trade-union pressure for higher wages may be to some extent simply a by-product of their efforts to get more members, and that when all industries are 100 per cent unionized, with no demarcation disputes or competitive membership drives, the pressure for higher wages may diminish.)

In any case, it is clear that even if the power of labour to raise wages and any resulting attempt by employers to raise prices is severely limited in any one industry by supply and demand conditions, the situation is different if there are many wages and prices rising simultaneously—*i.e.*, a condition of general inflation. Wage claims in a number of industries simultaneously or in close succession may, in the absence of government intervention, stand a better chance of success than in one industry, with "other things equal". Wage increases add to the pull of effective demand and so make it easier for employers to raise prices, while price increases by employers, even if not necessarily resulting from wage increases, also raise the incomes of the factors of production (unless all of the revenue resulting from increased prices goes to undistributed profits, in which case it adds to the income of shareholders at some future date). This very simplified picture of the wage-price spiral provides the basis for a prices and incomes policy. It does not, of course, prove that such a policy is practicable.

In addition to incomes policy, there may be a case for further measures to reduce the monopoly power of trade unions during a period of chronic inflation. (There is undoubtedly a case for bringing certain aspects of trade-union behaviour, such as restrictions on entry and training, within the scope of restrictive practices legislation.) One possibility is to make agreements between trade unions and employers enforceable at the firm but not the industry level. The *rationale* of this is evident from the discussion of elasticity of demand in Chapter 4. Since the demand for any industry's product is (except in one-firm industries) always more inelastic than the demand for the product of any firm in that industry, an industry-wide wage claim may often encounter less resistance from employers than a wage claim in one firm. Simply, employers know that if the claim is conceded all their competitors will be equally affected and the net outcome is likely to leave unaffected market shares and, depending on the *industry's* elasticity of demand and cost curves, also profits.

Obviously an attempt to confine wage bargaining to firms rather than industries would encounter severe practical difficulties. It would be necessary to rule out collusion between trade unions in different firms. If not, simultaneous wage claims could be submitted; and the situation might even be worsened if trade unions decided to pick off employers one at a time. Under industry-wide bargaining the duration of strikes is limited by the size of union funds, while with wage bargaining confined to firms rather than industries trade unions might be able to undertake a series of strikes without serious financial losses.

4. *Limitations of pressure groups*

It has been suggested in the preceding section of this chapter that the monopoly power of trade unions is easily exaggerated, and that while wage claims may be a factor in rising prices there is no evidence that either individual trade unions or labour as a whole has been able to increase substantially their members' share of the national product. If this is true, and if the largest pressure group—labour—has been able to do little to influence its reward by organization, it may be suspected that an exaggerated view is often taken of the influence of pressure groups in general on the economic position of their members.

In fact, there are three cardinal limitations on the power of pressure groups. One is that most groups find themselves in conflict with opposing groups in society. The second is that pressure groups contain within themselves conflicting interests, and the larger the group the more likely it is to do so. Economic interests are objective, while the existence and scope of a pressure group is largely a matter of historical accident. The third is that the power of the government to disregard pressure is vast and probably increasing.

A French authority concludes: "What is generally forgotten or underestimated is that often an essential part of the activity of interest groups (and even of those groups which are non-economic and non-professional in character) is directed against other rival groups: beet growers against makers of alcohol, road haulage against rail transport, home distillers against commercial distillers, retailers against chain stores and co-operatives, and so on."[15] In industry the interests of industrial consumers conflict with their suppliers. All

[15] G. E. Lavau, *Political pressures in France*, in H. W. Ehrmann (ed.) *Interest Groups on Four Continents* (published for the International Political Science Association by the University of Pittsburgh Press, 1958), p. 65.

manufacturers would like cheap fuel and raw materials. Car manufacturers, if not producers of components themselves, will wish to buy them as cheaply as possible, perhaps from abroad. Shipping-lines will buy their ships abroad if domestic shipbuilders are seriously uncompetitive. Even consumer goods by the usual classification may be an input of an industry or trade—e.g., glass containers purchased by agriculture, cars for commercial travellers, and re-frigerators bought by hotels, catering establishments, and food re-tailers. Such considerations cannot be ignored by a government wishing to impose import restrictions on any of these requisites, and the purchasers concerned will plead that their competitiveness and foreign currency earnings will be adversely affected if they can-not buy in the cheapest market.

Since economic interests are objective, while the existence and scope of a pressure group is a matter of historical accident, it follows that a pressure group may contain conflicting interests. The Trades Union Congress, representing almost the entire labour force of the country, has to take account, in the event of a dispute between bus drivers or electricity workers and their employers, of the interests of other workers as consumers of bus services and electricity (not to mention the effect on the Labour Party's election prospects. The 1958 London bus strike is credited with an influence on the Party's losses in the General Election of the following year). Within an in-dustry there may be a conflict between skilled and unskilled workers.

> The interests of all union members, or even of different members of the same union, are by no means necessarily identical. The skilled railwayman who wants an equal percentage increase for all, and the unskilled man who wants an equal cash increase, can be in conflict; so can railwaymen generally, who get only their union rate, and engineers who get much more. Even before the union negotiator gets to the bargaining table, he will have had to sort out these conflicting claims. . . . Bargaining over these con-flicting opinions of members can often be a much more arduous task than bargaining with the employer.[16]

Another example of a conflict of interests within a group is that of cereals and livestock producers within the National Farmers' Union. The latter are users of grain as animal feed, and want prices to be kept low. As livestock producers account for about three-quarters of the value of agricultural output in Britain (and, as they are mainly

[16] G. Cyriax and R. Oakeshott, *The Bargainers* (Faber and Faber, 1960), pp. 169–70.

small farmers, an even greater percentage of votes within the N.F.U.) the farmers' organization is very wary of any measure which might lead to higher grain prices. In other countries, where cereals producers and livestock farmers often have separate organizations, the government has to carry out the reconciliation of interests which in Britain is carried out within the N.F.U. A large representative organization such as the Confederation of British Industry has to reconcile the conflicting interests of steel producers and consumers, fuel producers and consumers, manufacturers and retailers, and so on.

Governments often find that the objective political strength of pressure groups, when tested, is less than had been believed. A study of the political significance of the British agricultural vote concluded that

> On balance, our study supports the view expressed by other workers that the influence of the agricultural vote is extremely small nationally and assumes importance in only fourteen constituencies. . . . A programme that is pleasing to the agricultural vote could result in a few seats being won, but such a programme might well displease a far larger section of the community and could result in many other seats being lost.[17]

Another significant fact is that leaders of groups may adopt a position out of touch with the views or actions of their members; it was observed in Britain during the furore over the introduction of trading stamps on a large scale in 1963–64 that most of the members of the organizations which were vociferously denouncing trading stamps were at the time giving trading stamps. (This point is also of significance for a consumer pressure group; it may be difficult to establish whether the view of a "political" consumers' organization in fact represents the views of all or most consumers. Opinion surveys are of limited value, as consumers, unfortunately, sometimes indicate different preferences by their shopping behaviour to those expressed in interviews.)

Some argue that government concessions to a small producer group can win the votes of that group, and that the losses, spread over the whole community, may go unnoticed. This is rather doubt-

[17] V. H. Beynon and J. E. Harrison, University of Exeter, Department of Economics (Agricultural Economics) Report No. 134, July 1962, pp. 30–31. (In the U.S.A. and perhaps in some other countries the political strength of agriculture is increased by the over-representation of rural areas in Congress.)

ful. It does not appear to be true that a rise in price of an item which is significant in terms of percentage of consumers' expenditure will result in no loss of political popularity. The British Government of 1964 discovered that a rise in the price of even a fairly minor item like beef will attract obloquy if the public at large regards it as a traditional and essential one in its standard of living. Public demand for action may be misguided (most frequently a demand for price control) but the fact remains that a government which halted the price rise, by whatever means, would gain considerably in popularity. On the other hand it may well be true that failure by a government to take action which could bring about price *reductions* (*e.g.*, tariff cuts, or permitting competition in sectors where it is at present restricted, such as, in Britain, bus transport) will fail to attract attention, since the public may fail to appreciate that the possibility existed.

The view, common to certain classical economists[18] and Marxists, that there is an inevitable conflict between the interests of sectional groups and those of society as a whole, is not accepted. Not much can be said in general terms as to whether such a conflict exists; as with monopoly, case study is needed. If education ought to be expanded the efforts of teachers to secure more money for education are praiseworthy; in spending on roads, so are the efforts of the Roads Campaign Council. If it is desirable to expand agricultural production for balance of payments reasons the farmers' organizations are working in the national interest as well as their own by lobbying for this objective (though only if they devise a means of expanding production which is of optimum benefit to the balance of payments).

The tactics adopted, also, will depend as much on what society believes to be tolerable as on the group concerned, and it may well be that an inefficient pressure group, or one which has a misguided view of its own interests (*e.g.*, the view of some manufacturers in the inter-war period that high levels of unemployment were needed for industry to function efficiently) may be much more disastrous than a reverse case. It is neither unreasonable nor impracticable to induce a group to take a long-term view of its own interests, as shown, for example, by experience in Western Europe during the

[18] See quotation from Adam Smith at the head of this chapter. (In fairness to Adam Smith, it should be noted that he says the interests of traders is always "in some respects" different from that of the public.)

F

development of the Common Market. Industrial interests, having been persuaded that the formation of a Common Market was in the interest of the economy as a whole, accepted the short-term losses involved, with the help of transitional aids such as compensation to labour for redundancy or to factory owners for switching to other products. Similarly, it might be reasonable in its own interests for a trade union, once it had become convinced that demand for labour in its sector was falling, to concentrate its energies on compensation for redundancy and provision of re-training. In the same way small retailers, rather than trying to persuade the government to place obstacles in the way of the development of multiple chains and supermarkets—as they have done in some European countries, to the great detriment of efficiency in retailing—might be induced to increase their own efficiency, particularly by forming buying groups, and by utilizing their natural advantages of location, flexible opening hours, and personal service. But from the standpoint of the sectional group concerned it could be argued that so long as there is a good prospect of persuading the government to adopt restrictive measures, re-organization to adapt to changing conditions should take second place. Here again it may be seen that the tactics adopted by the group depend more on outside constraints than on its own volition, and that the task for the policy maker is to create the institutional framework in which a sectional interest has to take adaptive rather than restrictive measures.

6

Consumers' Countervailing Power

The growth of resale price maintenance during the last half-century is one of several developments in industry and trade which have operated against the interests of consumers. In my view the subordination of the interests of consumers to those of producers (both public and private) has gone so far that a reversal of the trend is highly desirable.

B. S. YAMEY[1]

1. *A consumer pressure group?*

Reasons have been set out in the preceding chapter for regarding the growth and proliferation of organized interest groups of producers with some equanimity. To recapitulate briefly, these are: (1) pressure groups often contain conflicting interests within their own ranks and their power is offset by opposing groups in the economy; (2) the extent to which pressure groups such as trade associations, trade unions, and professional organizations can interfere with the working of supply and demand is very limited unless they can control entry into the trade or profession or they can restrict the activities of competitors; (3) pressure groups must, at least ostensibly, harmonize their objectives and the public interest; (4) despite the growth of pressure groups, governments are in a strong position to over-ride them in the national interest; (5) pressure groups sometimes arise from a deterioration in the economic status of a particular group, and in these cases there may be something to be said for them on grounds of equity; (6) economic interests exist, and are liable to conflict, quite irrespective of the existence of pressure groups. To these considerations may be added (7) certain groups—*e.g.*, in Britain council-house tenants and

---

[1] *The Economics of Resale Price Maintenance* (Sir Isaac Pitman and Sons, London, 1954), p. 129.

ex-public schoolboys, have achieved positions of economic privilege without anything resembling a formal pressure group.

In applying these considerations to the position of the consumer, the first question which presents itself is why a deterioration in the economic position of consumers, as indicated by the continuous rise in prices since the Second World War, has not set off the counter-movement predicated in (5) above. The answer is that, to some extent, it has; an undoubted factor in the progress of the consumer movement in nearly all advanced countries since the early 1950's has been the steady rise in prices. In the same way the more objectionable forms of advertising and high-pressure salesmanship have assisted the growth of the consumer movement by a reaction among the more intelligent strata of the population. However, more important is that as mentioned previously "pure" consumers are few in number and weak in bargaining power, and for the great mass of the population it is both easier and, from their own point of view, more rational to concentrate on improving their position as producers rather than as consumers. (Even the non-producer groups who constitute "pure" consumers—the retired, the sick, the unemployed, the idle rich—will probably find it more fruitful to try to improve their position by political bargaining or other means than to improve their position as consumers.)

It follows from (6) above that it is not always necessary for consumers to have a formal pressure group in order to exert more influence, nor is a formal organization necessarily the best means. For example, excessive power on the part of one producer group may best be countered by increasing the influence of commercial purchasers from the group, increasing the scope of other groups in competition with the group, or eliminating obstacles to the entry of new producers into the industry or trade concerned. In practical terms, in many cases the best way of strengthening consumers may be, for example, monopolies and restrictive practices legislation, or increasing the number of people undergoing professional or technical training. One of the main tasks of organizations set up to represent consumers' interests at the political level, such as the Prices and Incomes Board in Britain, should be to isolate those cases where no effective pressures on the producer side exist to limit the power of certain industries (there is here obviously a good deal of overlap with monopoly legislation) or groups, to ascertain whether counter-pressures can be increased and whether counter-pressure by consumers would have a chance of success.

Although we have argued in Chapter 4 that there is no distinctive category of "administered prices" to which particular attention should be devoted, the need for investigations on the lines of the Monopolies Commission must form a considerable part of consumer counter-pressure. In addition, there is a category of prices which might be described as "political". This group is not clear-cut; the main examples are probably agriculture, and industries with a high degree of tariff or non-tariff protection against imports. An appropriately constituted consumer pressure group might be able to achieve something if represented at the annual agricultural price review. Where tariff cases are concerned the Board of Trade is enjoined to take the consumer interest into account, but it will normally consider a reduction in a particular tariff only as part of international negotiations, or if a specific request has been made by an organization representing users. Hitherto there has been no organization submitting requests for tariff reductions on behalf of the final consumer.

Such work might follow logically the Consumers' Association's comparative testing. Where a foreign product has been found to be superior and/or is lower in price than the domestic product, and the latter is protected by a high tariff, a strong case could be made out. Cameras and watches come to mind as cases where the original reason for high tariff protection (imposed for defence reasons soon after the First World War) is almost completely obsolete, where tests by *"Which?"* have shown some British products to be inferior, and where prices of comparable foreign products are often lower. In actively seeking out cheap foreign sources of supply, a consumer organization would have the support of retailers, wholesalers, and importers, who already do this but are handicapped as regards negotiations with government departments by their small size, and lack of organization (as compared with, say, the National Coal Board, the Electricity Boards, and farmers). Where there are no tariff or non-tariff barriers to imports, the interests of wholesalers, retailers, and importers should usually be adequate to find the cheapest source of supply, although lack of information may prevent them from doing so.

As a national consumer organization of this kind would give the appearance of being unpatriotic, it would be preferable for combined testing, price comparison, and tariff-reduction studies to be done internationally, when it would generally be found that criticism of one country's product in one field was balanced by criticism of another country's in a different field. An international consumer organization of this kind could usefully work in conjunction with the General Agreement on Tariffs and Trade, which itself badly needs the help of such a pressure group.

Consumer representation in nationalized industries (considered in Chapter 8) and on international commodity control schemes provides some indication of the usefulness and limitations of the appointment of consumer "representatives". Anticipating the conclusions of Chapter 8, we may note that the results of consumer representation in nationalized industries in Britain have been slight, partly because of the concentration on consumer complaints rather than on prices and partly because of the limited resources of the consumer bodies and their dependence on the industries concerned. In general, it may be said that the more the industry concerned is subject to the forces of competition the less need there is for direct consumer representation, though the two are not of course mutually exclusive.

In the existing (post-1945) international commodity control schemes set up under United Nations auspices producer and consumer countries have equal representation, but producers usually have the power to act unilaterally on the crucial questions of price and production control. Indeed, in the absence of such a provision equal representation of consumers would simply lead to deadlock in cases of disagreement. It is difficult to see any solution, except possibly by the consumer representatives widening their ambit to include alternative supplies (*e.g.*, competing materials, or producers outside the scheme) and promoting these if a price or production agreement is considered unreasonable. In practice, the solution may be to modify or abolish the agreement. The power of international commodity schemes to raise prices is in any case severely limited, except where production is concentrated in the hands of a small number of countries and there are no close substitutes. Perhaps the closest to such a case is the international tin agreement, but even here the power to raise prices is limited by the desire of low-cost producers (Malaya) to expand their share of the market and by the (increasing) substitutability of other raw materials for tin.

From this discussion and the preceding one it will be evident no great hopes are to be placed on the setting up of organizations to "represent" consumers politically. Appointing consumers' representatives to sit on government committees, boards of State industries, or private firms, is of limited value. *Producers'* views are listened to respectfully not because they are represented politically but because of their expertise and their power to make their opinions felt. "Consumer representation" may be a retrograde step if it is assumed that in itself it solves any problems. It can only do this if, first, consumer representatives have economic, scientific, and technical knowledge to make their views carry equal weight with those of producers (in practice, this means that consumer representative bodies can only be as good as their research staff); if they can use sanctions against those who oppose them; and if they have the power to influence the views of those they represent.

2. *A consumers' strike?*

If not much faith is to be placed in political organizations for the representation of consumers, we may examine some "non-political" possibilities.

If, as is sometimes argued, the strength of trade unions lies largely in their power to strike, the possibility of a consumers' strike would seem to be relevant. Discussions and threats of such a measure have been frequent in the post-war period—*e.g.*, by the (Conservative) politically-inspired Housewives' League which was active in the latter days of the Labour Government of 1945–51. In France there have been a number of attempts to bring down the price of particular products, notably meat, by abstention from buying. There were attempts at local boycotts of particular grocery products which had risen in price in Britain in 1966–68. In the same period housewives' boycotts were undertaken in the U.S.A., partly with the objective of forcing chain stores and supermarkets to cut prices rather than use sales promotion methods such as trading stamps, with local, if temporary, successes, and with modified support from the President's Special Adviser on Consumer Affairs.

Detailed proposals for strike action by consumers has been put forward in *The Consumers' Manifesto* by Mario Pei[2] (a Professor of Languages at Columbia University). Pei argues that as consumer and producer interests coincide much less than employers' and labour interests, it is usually in the interests of employers and labour to combine against the consumer (this is essentially Galbraith's picture of what happens during a period of inflation). He concludes

[2] Crown Publishers Inc., New York, 1960.

that consumers must organize in the same way as a trade union and that this should adopt the usual means, including strike action, of promoting its members' interests. "The organizational methods of the United Consumers of America should be patterned after those of the better-run labour unions, of which there are a great number that can be used as models of both democratic and efficient operation."[3] The main task of the proposed consumers' union, as envisaged by Mario Pei, would be to examine labour-management disputes as they arise, and U.C.A. representatives would sit in on the negotiations and judge the validity of the opposing claims. For example, it is usual for management in such situations to claim that profits are not high enough to enable them to grant a wage demand, while the labour side claims that they are. U.C.A. would try to judge these claims by reference to profit and cost figures, the market situation and prospects, and so on. It would then declare itself for one or the other of the two sides to the dispute, and try to get its recommendations adopted. In the event of one of the two sides not accepting its recommendations, it would declare the firm or union concerned "black" and organize a consumer boycott of its products. A war chest would be held to compensate consumer members for any losses they might suffer as a result of a boycott of the products of a particular firm or union, though the strike weapon would, as in ordinary industrial negotiations, be used only as a last resort. It would not be necessary, for the strike to be successful, for U.C.A. to include 100 per cent of consumers, nor would it be necessary for all members to adhere to its recommendations; only that they should do so in sufficient numbers to make a substantial dent in the profits or wages of the "black" firm or union.

Despite the very limited results of any actions to date, the use of the strike weapon by consumers probably deserves further study. To the objection that it offers scope for commercial blackmail—for instance, by competitors of the firm against which a strike was directed—it may be replied that so does the strike weapon when used *against* consumers. However, there do appear to be severe practical difficulties. A strike against a particular firm or product might be feasible, but it is difficult to see how consumers could strike against a particular trade union, except in the case of a one-firm union, and even in this case the firm (who, if the trade union are in the wrong in the dispute, may be assumed to be in the right) would

[3] *op. cit.*, p. 31.

be damaged as much as the union. More fundamentally, it is likely that there would always be a large number of consumer "blacklegs" who were unwilling to join the strike, as the potential gains at stake are, from the point of view of the individual consumer, so small compared with the inconvenience of striking as to make a high degree of consumer solidarity unlikely.

Professor Pei envisages a consumer strike being used in the case of labour-management disputes which have adverse effects on consumers. But it is not clear that consumers' representatives would usually have any competence to pronounce on the issues involved. As far as price increases are concerned, it is later argued (Chapters 11 and 12) that it is extremely difficult to lay down criteria by which particular increases can be judged justified or unjustified, especially at a time of general inflation when many prices are rising simultaneously. However, there seem to be no fundamental reasons, either practical or of principle, why consumers' boycotts could not be organized with specific and limited objectives, such as deceptive trading practices by producers or certain kinds of restrictive practices by employees (a minor if ever-topical example is the practice of No. 11 buses of London Transport of running in convoys; conceivably a consumer boycott of the route might force the practice to be dropped).

In summary, the prospects for substantial results from a consumers' strike are not at the present time very great. However, the essential idea involved is the same as that which underlies most consumer protection measures—*i.e.*, to enable consumers to react more strongly against price increases. (In economic terms, to make the demand curve for particular products more elastic.) If there is adequate consumer information and effective competition between producers, consumers can react more strongly against an increase in the price of a particular product or brand. The same applies to consumer education, weights and measures legislation, action against deceptive trading practices and misleading advertising, and the whole range of "consumer protection" measures.

3. *Broadening the range of alternatives*

Self-evidently, the larger the range of alternatives open to the consumer, the greater his power to react against price increases. The most important measures here are those designed to increase competition. Product innovation is also, obviously, a major factor in broadening the range of alternatives open to the consumer. There

are less obvious means. Three typical possibilities are discussed
below.

(1) An interesting proposal has been put forward by an economist
with practical knowledge of the retail furniture trade[4] which might
be extended, suitably modified, to other branches of retailing and
the service industries. The author holds that in the retail furniture
trade "Comparison between goods in different shops is deliberately
made difficult. . . . The range of furniture is so wide that similar,
but distinct articles can always be substituted for anything which is
ostensibly in direct competition. Moreover, no retailer likes price
competition, so that no one [engages in it] for fear of retaliation."
Once the customer is inside the shop

> a campaign of aggressive salesmanship starts. A salesman is
> accounted a failure if a potential customer is allowed to escape
> without placing an order. This has the effect of frightening the
> customers from entering the shop until they are prepared to buy
> there. Yet the only means of forming a judgment lies through
> window displays and advertising matter provided by the retailers.
> Since the margins added to those goods which are advertised or
> displayed are, in many instances, much lower than those ruling
> throughout the shop the customer cannot find value for money
> simply by looking from the outside.

The conclusion which the author draws from his study of a chain-
type furniture shop in a working-class district is that

> By and large, competition is ineffective. In the first place, the field
> of competition is narrowed through the existence of a class
> shopping structure. Secondly, consumers are not adequately in-
> formed as to the relative value of household goods and are there-
> fore not good judges of value. Thirdly, retailers seek, and are able,
> to avoid direct competition, and, fourthly, hire-purchase has
> created a strong demand which is not sensitive to price com-
> petition. As an experiment, it would be interesting to see the
> establishment of a town market in household goods with retailers
> competing side by side under the same roof. This would allow
> the shopper better opportunities of inspection before buying. At
> present, however, one cannot escape the conclusion that the con-
> sumer, and particularly the working class consumer, is the victim
> of undesirable trading practices.

In part, the problem is the perennial one of bringing adequate con-

[4] J. G. Morell, "Furniture for the masses", *Journal of Industrial Economics*,
November 1956.

sumer information to the working-class buyer. In part, it stems from the nature of the product; furniture is one of a group of products where information cannot easily be given by means of comparative testing and labelling. It is therefore important that shopping facilities should be arranged to make point-of-sale comparisons easy. Since the siting of shops is largely influenced by town planning authorities, there is a great deal to be said for Morell's suggestion for placing shops selling the same product under a single roof. (In certain, especially non-city, areas there is also, however, a case for dispersing shops to make them easily accessible. These two propositions are not necessarily contradictory; together they indicate the need for as large a number of shops as is economically feasible; or, in practical terms, the undesirability of measures such as licensing—as in some European countries—or the Selective Employment Tax in Britain, which may limit the number of shops.)

(2) It is a familiar feature of retailing that in supermarkets price cuts are concentrated on particular items and are not spread equally "across the board". This is a legitimate promotional technique. The reason appears to be that housewives notice a large price reduction, but may not notice a large number of small price reductions. "Housewives can compare only a limited number of lines. They have accurate ideas of the normal price only of a very few lines."[5] It may however result in a certain amount of confusion, and also the shopper may have to make a considerable effort—including travelling—if she is to take advantage of the different price cuts prevailing in different shops. A solution could be found in a collective shopping technique, evolved in California. Women pool their weekly orders, and from the advertised "special bargains" they select the supermarket offering the lowest price on each item. They divide up the combined order, and one woman shops at Supermarket A, another at Supermarket B, and so on. Afterwards they settle their accounts between themselves.[6]

Here again, part of the answer lies in consumer information. Certain local consumer groups in Britain, notably Crawley, have experimented in posting the prices of major items in supermarkets, race-course fashion, on a board in the centre of the town. Another

[5] W. G. McClelland, *Studies in Retailing* (Basil Blackwell, Oxford, 1963), p. 31. (The reference is to genuine price cutting, not fictitious price cutting, or "double pricing".)

[6] International Co-operative Alliance, *Consumer Affairs Bulletin*, No. 2, 1963.

possible means of making price comparisons easier would be to persuade supermarkets to advertise collectively in a local newspaper their current price-lists for a number of products, publishing the advertisements side by side. Such informational work could no doubt be undertaken by a local consumer group but it would be better if retailers could be induced to do it.

(3) Other than monopoly and restrictive practices legislation, the most effective means of increasing competition probably lies in promoting alternatives which are not immediately obvious as such, and which are not closely connected industry-wise. Thus the need for transport to work can be reduced by close control at the local level over the location of employment *vis-à-vis* residential development. The need for transport to visit shops can also be reduced in this way (*e.g.*, if there are adequate shops widely dispersed in residential areas; excessively rigid town-planning restrictions have hindered this development in Britain). Transport requirements for holidays and for recreational purposes could be reduced if urban areas were made more pleasant places to live in—but here we impinge on the needs of the citizen rather than the consumer, and do not pursue the matter further.

Efficient service industries will increase the degree of competition for certain types of manufacturers, and vice versa. If the consumer can get his car or television set or clothing repaired easily and cheaply the manufacturer of these items will be less secure in his prospects of replacement sales; and efficient durable-goods manufacturing industries reduce the consumer's reliance on repairs and servicing and thus bring competitive pressure to bear on these sectors of the service trades.

4. *Low-cost alternatives*

The market mechanism, if unhindered by price agreements between producers, and in particular resale price maintenance, usually presents the consumer with a wide range of price and quality. In recent years retailers' brands—largely unadvertised—have provided a wide range of low-cost alternatives to heavily advertised manufacturers' brands. The most spectacular cases have been in chemists' goods, but examples are also to be found in clothing, groceries, and household cleaning products. In other cases, perhaps simply through failure to perceive their own interests, producers may have failed to market potential low-cost alternatives. "A few years ago there was such a thing as the model-T car, which was hundreds of dollars cheaper than its rivals. Today there is no counterpart of this classic vehicle, nor can one buy a phone on a 50-party line."[7]

The most important example of a low-cost alternative which is in danger of having its availability seriously reduced is public transport, and the limitations it places on the need or desire to purchase private passenger transport; however, the transport problem poses such wide questions that it cannot be further pursued here. Public policy often unintentionally reduced the availability of low-price alternatives. Street markets are sometimes endangered by unimaginative enforcement of town-planning regulations. Enforcement of minimum-quality standards may reduce the availability of low-cost products. In Britain the Parker-Morris Committee report ("Homes for Today and Tomorrow") of 1961 made recommendations—which have been widely adopted by local authorities in their building programmes, though not yet in the private sector despite pressure from well-meaning organizations—which it has been estimated would have added at prices then prevailing some £300 to the cost of a three-bedroom house. Minimum-quality standards should not be enforced unless there are clear questions of health and safety involved. In addition, proposals for licensing or registering trades such as plumbers, hairdressers, estate agents, travel agents, etc., usually aim at restricting freedom of entry and so raising prices, on the pretext of raising standards. However, as the ostensible aim is probably not often realized, such proposals are not of much relevance in this context.

Producers can usually find plausible reasons for removing low-cost alternatives from the market, often claiming that they are of unacceptably low quality, or dangerous. A classic instance is the British Egg Marketing Board's withdrawal of egg "seconds". "Seconds" are fresh eggs tendered to the Egg Board through packing stations and rejected as ineligible for government subsidy because they have cracked shells or other faults which are revealed during the grading process. The price of "seconds" varies according to locality but is often about half that of first-quality eggs. The Egg Marketing Board, while admitting that one of the objectives of the scheme was to raise the price of first-quality eggs, claimed that the

[7] Ruby Turner Norris, *The Theory of Consumers' Demand* (Yale University Press, 1941), pp. 181–182. Other possibilities suggested by Professor Norris are paperback editions of best-sellers published simultaneously with the hard-cover editions, a cheap newspaper of only a few pages, and cigarettes sold in bulk at so much per pound.

scheme would also "ensure that only first-quality eggs and egg products would reach the consumer or user" and that it would "remove from human consumption eggs and egg products which may be dangerous to health".[8]

The Consumers' Committee for England and Wales, the statutory organization set up to represent consumers *vis-à-vis* the agricultural marketing boards, disputed all these claims and pointed out the hardship which would ensue if cheap eggs were no longer marketed, especially for pensioners, the unemployed, and large families. Despite this opposition, the scheme was carried through. A feature of this and similar schemes by producers is that established retailers do not oppose them very vigorously, as they might be expected to do in terms of Galbraithian countervailing power, for the reason that the low-cost product is sold to a considerable extent through unorthodox retail outlets (in this case, street markets). In other cases inertia, inefficiency, or the feeling that all retailers will be equally affected, so that none would lose a competitive advantage by discontinuing the cheap product, may be equally potent reasons for lack of action.

5. *Increasing competition*

In a sense, if the term "competition" is stretched widely enough, several of the policies discussed in this book could be incorporated in a programme for increasing competition (broadening the range of alternatives, low-cost alternatives, consumer information). But as "competition policy" has a well-defined traditional usage in economics, limited in the main to questions relating to "monopoly" (absolute or relative size) and restrictive practices, it seems desirable to discuss these new policy proposals under a different heading.

As mentioned, several countries have recently made tariff cuts, occasionally unilateral, to counter price increases. In agriculture and manufacturing the importance of actual or potential competition from imports can hardly be exaggerated. An increase in imports is also a powerful deflationary weapon in the macro-economic context

[8] Consumers' Committee for Great Britain, *Report on the Operation of the British Egg Marketing Scheme, 1956*, June 1964. The next *Report*, in February 1968, commented: "It is possible that imported eggs have to some extent compensated for the withdrawal of seconds near ports. It is of interest that the Board released seconds on to the retail market for a short period towards the end of 1966, notwithstanding the opinions which the Board had previously expressed about the health hazards from these eggs."

(the same amount of money chasing a larger amount of goods, to use an over-simplified but fairly apt characterization of the inflationary process). Conversely, an export surplus, other things being equal, has an inflationary impact on an economy, and statements about the need for an export surplus of specified or unspecified size should be scrutinized with rather more care than they sometimes receive.

Foreign investment can stimulate competition. It is consistently found in manufacturing industry that American firms operating in Britain make higher profits than British firms in the same industry, because of lower costs. In France, where retailing and advertising are not well developed, encouragement of foreign (*e.g.* U.S. or British) firms in these sectors would be one of the most effective ways of modernizing them.

Foreign investment apart, it is difficult to intensify competition in the service sector, which takes a steadily increasing share of consumers' spending, investment, and the labour force in advanced countries. "In forty years the number of Americans engaged in producing commodities has hardly changed. The entire increase in the work-force has gone into what can broadly be called services of all kinds: there are many more taxi-drivers, salesmen, bankers, barbers, doctors, teachers, insurance agents and restauranteurs for example, and as will surprise no one, many, many more people employed by government."[9] According to one estimate, 80 per cent of the labour force in the U.S.A. will be employed in the service sector by the end of the century, and only 20 per cent in agriculture, manufacturing, and mining combined. Similar if slower trends are at work in other countries.

As noted, because of imports "enforced" competition is more easily attainable in manufacturing, agriculture, or mining—no matter how inefficient or restrictive domestic producers are—than in retailing, wholesaling, and the service sector generally. Comparative testing and labelling, also, cannot be used to promote competition in the service sector. There are two further reasons for paying special attention to the retail trade. There is an unavoidable element of local monopoly in retailing; and the retail trade and many other service trades sell to the final rather than the intermediate consumer and are therefore less subject to pressure from well-informed, full-time buyers.

[9] C. W. McMahon and G. D. N. Worswick, "The growth of services in the economy", *District Bank Review*, December 1960. p. 3.

It follows that it is important not to discourage or restrict entry by new firms or individuals into the service sector. In the professions, restrictions imposed by the professional organizations are deservedly coming under closer scrutiny.

Special attention should be paid to all forms of "by-passing" selling, and resistance offered to any restrictions in retailing—for example, the recurrent proposal to restrict sales of pharmaceuticals to chemists' shops. The element of danger in selling non-prescription chemists' goods through non-specialist shops, and the amount of useful advice provided to the public by pharmacists, were both shown at the Restrictive Practices Court hearings to be negligible.[10] The degree of specialization in retailing could probably be further reduced. For example, there seems no good reason why practically all retail outlets should not sell newspapers, in which trade it appears, despite some agreements having been condemned by the Restrictive Practices Court, an informal "distance limit" policy is still in force in some areas. Trade restrictions on wholesalers acting as retailers (which were also prevalent at one time in the newspaper trade—it is not clear whether they still exist) need to be particularly guarded against. In the U.S.A. and Canada some of the most notable advances in retailing have come about through wholesalers opening retail outlets.

Mail order, mobile shops, automatic vending machines, and door-to-door selling (the latter freed of its element of high-pressure coercive selling, at least in Britain, by recent legislation which gives the customer a "cooling-off" period to reconsider his decision to buy) should be, if not artificially encouraged, at least protected from avoidable obstacles. Retailers' attempts to prevent manufacturers or others from selling direct to the public, which at present are frequent and successful, should be illegal. For example, a report in *The Grocer* in 1964 cited the action taken over a customer who bought food direct from the manufacturer.

The customer . . . had been given a deep-freeze cabinet by her husband and usually had ten to twelve packs of frozen foods a

[10] Mr Justice (now Lord) Devlin, giving judgment in the Chemists' Federation case, said: "We believe that the vast majority of proprietary medicines sold by chemists are sold over the counter, frequently by unqualified assistants, without any inquiry being made, just in the same way as they are in drug stores or general shops, and that it has never up till now occurred to anyone to think that there is a real risk of injury in the process." (All-England Law Reports, 1958, Vol. 3, p. 458.)

week from her grocer. When she did not make her usual order the retailer asked her why and she said she had made arrangements through Findus who were delivering direct to her. "If people are supplied at the same price as us it is a serious matter . . ." the Federation president commented. "This will have to be watched for it is a situation which will grow."[11]

In our columns recently there appeared a report of a complaint by a (local Meat Trades) Association meeting that meat was being sold direct to a consumer from the abbatoir. As a result of investigation by the Association the practice ceased. This case provides an excellent illustration of the strength and influence that can be exerted in defence of the individual in return for the small subscription that membership of our organization entails. Unfortunately the servicing of consumers direct from the wholesale market or abbatoir is not new to our trade. . . .[12]

In parts of the retail and service field, there may be scope for trading intervention by local, regional, or national government. A survey of municipal trading in Britain and elsewhere, its successes as well as its failures, would be a useful starting-point. So long as the State enterprise covers its costs and is not subsidized in any way there can be no legitimate grounds for complaint by private business. It is a remarkable feature of ideologically influenced economic thinking that those economists who argue most strongly the need for increased competition are usually unwilling to countenance extensive competition from State or municipal enterprise.

The National Coal Board, the Milk Marketing Board, and other agricultural producers' organizations could usefully undertake more wholesale and retail operations than at present. The M.M.B. operates five successful retail outlets but has apparently been deterred from further expansion in retailing by the need to keep on good terms with private distributors and retailers. The N.C.B. has a small part of the wholesale and retail coal trade, a perceptible share of the brick manufacturing industry, and has recently expressed the intention of making some welcome forays into the building industry. In many countries agricultural organizations are being forced to examine the efficiency of the distributive chain and occasionally to take steps to remedy the defects. If they do not take such action complaints by them about inefficiency or high profits in distribution of agricultural products are not very convincing.

The removal of restrictions on shop opening hours, and longer

[11] *The Grocer*, August 1st, 1964.
[12] Editorial in the *Meat Trades Journal*, September 25th, 1962. p. 797.

G

opening hours for associated institutions such as banks and post-offices, would increase competition in the retail sector, not least by allowing consumers to shop at off-peak hours when they could do so more carefully. It should not be necessary to add that longer shop opening hours do not mean longer working hours for retail workers; employers could adopt more shift-working and make more extensive use of part-time labour.

6. *Bulk buying*

Bulk buying by consumers, and the varied and somewhat inequitable ways in which employees of certain firms and members of certain organizations can get "discounts" from specified employers, need to be studied and perhaps publicized, encouraged, and imitated.

Where the individual consumer is concerned, buying in bulk has obvious practical limits. However, *Which?* and *Shopper's Guide*[13] both concluded that for many products it was more economic to buy large-size than small packs (to be expected with most packaged goods, in view of the large proportion of the total cost which consists of packaging costs). The problem here is simply a "weights and measures" one; if the consumer knows the price and quantity of both the small and large sizes it is easy to work out which is better value for money.

Even when bulk buying is cheaper, there may be offsetting factors. Some items—*e.g.*, unprocessed food, salt—deteriorate when stored (though others, such as some wines, and sardines, improve). Many homes do not have much storage space, and as space becomes more expensive it is unlikely that this situation will improve (though ergonomics may make a contribution). Despite these problems, bulk buying should be encouraged as far as possible. One of the organizations selling in this fashion in Britain, the John Dron organization, claims that savings of 6 shillings in the pound are possible on many commodities including detergents, household cleaners, and household textiles. The organization claims to offer to the private consumer savings equivalent to those offered to large-scale buyers of these items, such as schools, colleges, hotels, restaurants, and clubs.

Some firms' employees (for example, car workers) are able to buy the firm's product at a reduced price. By logical extension, em-

[13] See, *e.g.*, *Which?*, December 1959, on detergents; *Shopper's Guide*, December 1960, on face cream.

ployees of some large organizations and members of some trade unions and professional bodies are able to buy at "trade" prices.[14] The usual justification for this practice is that the organization may itself be a large buyer of certain items—e.g., food or detergents, and may secure a discount on its purchases, though it is less easy to see the *rationale* of allowing members to secure discounts on goods not bought by the organization. This is not a criticism of discount schemes; quite the contrary—to the extent that economies of large-scale buying and a relatively assured market allow the supplier to offer lower prices, it follows that anyone who so wishes, and can bring together the necessary number of customers, should be able to form or join such an organization.

Large-scale buying has enabled chain stores, co-operatives, and other commercial purchasers to obtain lower prices from suppliers. Equally, it could be said that the discounts offered by suppliers have provided buyers with an incentive to bulk their purchases; the process is a desirable one, however it is looked at. Nor does it matter much *how* the discount is regarded as having been caused, whether by promoting economies in production, by guaranteeing "long runs", or simply by exerting bargaining power—*i.e.*, by threatening to buy elsewhere. For this reason, legislation such as the Robinson-Patman Act in the U.S.A., designed to prevent suppliers from offering discounts to large customers, is misguided and harmful to the extent that it is enforceable. Mainly it is the result of political pressure by small retailers.

The Co-operative movement has failed conspicuously to obtain the buying advantages secured by large retailers, owing to the autonomy of the individual retail societies and consequent failure to utilize the movement's collective buying power. Largely because of pressure from the smaller co-operative retail societies, the Co-operative Wholesale Societies as buying agents have not hitherto been able to offer substantial discounts to induce retail societies to order in bulk, and merge their orders. The (Gaitskell) Commission on the Co-operatives said that "the present system encourages driblet orders and uneconomic wholesaling methods", and recommended that the Wholesale Societies should "establish an open and generous system of volume discounts on all goods (including goods which are invoiced-through)".[15]

[14] See "Discount Trading", *Which?*, June 1959.
[15] *Co-operative Independent Commission Report*, Co-operative Union, 1959, p. 204.

The largest gains might come directly or indirectly from the purchasing power of national and local government. During discussions on the subject of school uniforms held by the Consumer Council in 1963–64 it emerged that the main problem facing suppliers was that each school insisted on its own type of uniform, with colour and braid variations. Given a standard uniform, to which schools could add their individual badge (but not individual braiding), the large retail clothing chains would be able to supply school uniforms probably at substantially reduced prices.

The Ministry of Public Building and Works is probably the largest furniture buyer in the country, and has begun to use its purchasing power to stimulate rationalization in the industry. Furniture manufacturing is, for the most part, made up of a large number of small firms which are under-capitalized, producing too wide a range of products, and are not equipped to take advantage of the latest productive techniques. Ministry efforts are now being devoted to concentrating demand on a smaller range of products and concentrating sources of supply, and may be expected to lead to lower prices both for government and private buyers. As far as the private consumer is concerned, this appears to be the first major development following the White Paper on *Public Purchasing and Industrial Efficiency* of May 1967.

Local authorities have in recent years bought or built about one-third of the annual housing output of the U.K. They have made only minor efforts to bulk their requirements and enforce standardization on builders and suppliers of components, or simply to force down building prices. If fully utilized, such power could have a revolutionary effect on the building industry and, despite the anomalies of council-house rents, would provide a justification for local authority involvement in housing and building. In school-building, consortia of local authorities have exerted just such an influence, with the result that the index of school-building costs has remained almost stable over the past decade while house-building costs have risen continuously.

7. *Consumer research*

Earlier in this chapter, a number of ways have been noted by which consumer economic research could be used to extend the effectiveness and range of consumer choice, for example research into consumer discounts and purchases at "trade" prices and into differences between domestic and foreign prices. Comparative testing (discussed in the next chapter) is the most important form of research designed to broaden the range of consumer choice.

Several other methods, besides comparative testing, could be used to uncover the most effective method of meeting given consumer wants or needs. A good example of the kind of research needed is a study by the Economic Research Service of the U.S. Department of Agriculture, *Comparative costs to the consumer of convenience foods and home produced foods*,[16] which revealed a much larger cost difference in favour of home-produced foods than had been expected. Some might argue that this is the kind of information which the consumer is well suited to ascertain for himself, not necessarily by making a conscious calculation; the evidence is, however, that he does not. The study does not prove that consumers should switch from convenience to home-produced foods, as the value of the time and effort spent on the latter will vary from individual to individual. Information such as in this study should be as widely disseminated as possible (it could suitably be included in school and college domestic economics courses).

Similar choices exist over most of the service field. Much of the growth of the service sector—laundries, restaurants, clothing repairs —may be regarded as a transfer to commercial organizations of work previously done within the family. In this, as well as in the substitutability of manufactured goods for many kinds of services, may lie the key to increasing the degree of price pressure on the service sector. No doubt the transfer of services from within the family to commercial organizations will continue, but it would intensify competition in the service sector if both consumers and suppliers of commercial services were widely aware of the possibilities of a re-transfer.

Little work has been done on the cost-effectiveness of different forms of heating, or on the possibilities, which appear to be extravagant, of reducing heating requirements by better building methods. There has been an intensive promotional campaign for different forms of central heating in Britain in recent years, and some attempt to assess for the benefit of consumers the cost of

[16] Economic Research Service of the U.S. Dept. of Agriculture, Marketing Research Report No. 609, June 1963, by H. M. Harp and D. F. Dunham. Convenience foods are defined as "foods that are partly or entirely prepared for serving by marketing agencies, which have a fresh or home-produced counterpart"—a rather wider definition than is normal as it would, for example, include bread. Normally the term is used to cover only the newer "convenience" foods.

different types and fuels, but mainly in newspaper articles and at a fairly unsophisticated level.[17] On this and similar subjects technical guidance should be available for consumers on payment of an appropriate fee. (The Building Research Station has done some of the necessary basic research.) Similar comparative research could be done on the costs of different types of passenger transport. As mentioned in the introductory chapter, it is a matter of urgency to provide information on the real costs of different types of consumer credit (though in this case little new *research* is needed) and, for example on the comparative costs of buying as compared with renting consumer durable goods, taking into account the costs of repair and maintenance.

All these kinds of research, designed to increase the efficiency of the consuming unit, need to be linked with information services to bring the results to as large a number of people as possible. The problem is in some respects similar—though more difficult, because of the larger number of recipient units—to that of increasing the efficiency of producers by management consultancy investigations, productivity campaigns, and so on. As an educational and public relations problem, it lies outside the scope of this book. However, the impact, in so far as it is measurable, of the present provision of consumer information and the possibilities of increasing this impact is the central problem of "consumer influence" and is one to which we now turn.

[17] One advanced study of the comparative costs of different systems of heating and different fuels is in the Parker-Morris Report, *Homes for Today and Tomorrow*, published by the Ministry of Housing and Local Government, 1961 (Appendix 2).

CHAPTER

7

Consumer Information and Organization

Now, who shall arbitrate?
Ten men love what I hate,
Shun what I follow, slight what I receive;
Ten who in ears and eyes
Match me: we all surmise,
They this thing, and I that: whom shall my soul believe?

ROBERT BROWNING
Rabbi ben Ezra

To spend money is easy, to spend it well is hard. Our faults
as spenders are not wholly due to wantonness, but largely to
broad conditions over which as individuals we have slight
control.

WESLEY C. MITCHELL[1]

1. *The rise of the consumer organizations*

In the middle years of the nineteenth century the Co-operative
movement was established in Britain with the aim of enabling
consumers to produce basic necessities for themselves and acquire
the profits from production and distribution. In many ways
this is a more radical and far-reaching aim than that of increasing
consumer influence *via* the price mechanism; but in most countries the consumer co-operative movement seems to have reached
a limit when it controls some 10 to 15 per cent of the retail trade
(and a much smaller proportion of manufacturing of consumer
goods). Recent developments in consumer protection have been
mainly due to initiative from outside the Co-operative movement.

The first organization to publish comparative test reports was

---

[1] *The Backward Art of Spending Money* (McGraw Hill, 1939), p. 4.

Consumer Research, set up in the U.S.A. in 1929 by F. J. Schlink.[2] He had published in 1927, jointly with Stuart Chase, a book called *Your Money's Worth* and circulated test reports privately for two years. Consumer Research now has an estimated 100,000 members who pay $4 a year for its monthly bulletin. This organization was soon overtaken by its competitor, Consumers' Union, formed in 1936, which has a circulation of over 900,000 for its monthly *Consumer Reports* at $6, though the *readership* is claimed by C.U. to be over 4 million.

Outside the U.S.A. the first comparable organization was the Danish Government Home Economics Council, established in 1935, financed in equal parts by the government and by sales of its bi-monthly bulletin (which is available to all, not only subscribers). Between 1948 and 1953 organizations for testing and labelling were set up in Sweden, France, and Switzerland. The latter may perhaps be taken as the date at which the consumer movement began its "take-off into self-sustained growth". In that year the Consumers' Union in Holland, the Working Group of Consumer Organizations (originally twelve women's, social, charitable, and Church organizations, and now comprising more than twenty) in West Germany, and the Norwegian Consumer Council, were set up. The Norwegian body is government-financed but independent. Test results, along with general advice and information, are published in its *Forbruker-raporten*, ten times a year. In 1960 this had a circulation of 15,000 but after a change to a more popular form and content its circulation rose to 100,000 five years later.

New consumer organizations were set up in Israel and Italy in 1955. In Britain, the first organization to undertake comparative testing was the Consumer Advisory Council of the British Standards Institution, which began publishing *Shopper's Guide* in March 1957. Seven months later the first issue of *Which?* was published by the Association for Consumer Research (later the name was changed to the Consumers' Association). *Which?*'s circulation rapidly overtook that of *Shopper's Guide*, and the latter ceased publication in 1963.

Consumer organizations were established in New Zealand and Australia in 1959 and in 1961 in Japan. The latter year was also marked by the appearance in Germany of a profit-making and

---

[2] Mr Schlink is still (1968) head of Consumer Research. He was opposed to trade unions, and it was as a result of this that some members of his staff broke away from C.R. and formed the now better-known Consumers' Union in 1936. Mr Schlink also opposed the New Deal, and held that consumers should make their own shoe polish, ink, cosmetics, and toothpaste.

advertisement-carrying consumer test publication, *Deustche Mark*, which in 1965 claimed a circulation of 500,000. The following year it ceased publication, but later re-appeared; while the West German Government set up a State Testing Institute for comparative test work in 1965.

An International Office (now the International Organization) of Consumers' Unions was set up in 1960 at The Hague to undertake the task of comparing test methods, and to undertake tests on an international scale, and the testing organizations of the six Common Market countries set up the Bureau Européen des Unions de Consommateurs in 1962 to carry out "Euro-tests" on a Community-wide basis.

2. *The impact of comparative test information*

Cases are on record where manufacturers have taken steps to improve their products following criticisms in *Which?* and other consumer magazines. In this way, comparative testing may lead directly to an improvement in productive efficiency.[3] Our concern here is the more fundamental effect it may have on consumers' buying decisions, and hence on the rate of expansion of the market share of the more efficient producers.

However, it is nearly impossible to find direct evidence of the effect of publication of test results on market shares, for much the same reason that it is in most cases impossible to isolate the effect of advertising or any other single factor on a producer's share of the market. Sales of individual manufacturers' products, and even more of individual brands, are usually closely guarded secrets.

In a few cases, sharp increases in sales are known to have followed a good rating in *Which?* After Sunbeam tricycles had been nominated a "Best Buy" in a guide to Christmas toys, retail stores had difficulty in keeping pace with the demand. Ronsons, manufacturer of an electric shaver, said that nomination of their brand as a B.B. had a "reasonable" effect on sales. In July 1963 *Which?* gave the Lec refrigerator a B.B. rating, and sales improved, but the product was already on an ascending sales curve. Olympia Business Machines said that nomination of their typewriter as a B.B. had

---

[3] The Molony Report (para. 379) said, apropos of comparative test reports: "Where faults of design, quality and sometimes safety have come to light, the reports have served to draw them imperatively to the manufacturer's attention. In these respects they have offered a valuable service, for which no other technique has provided or is likely to provide an adequate substitute."

little effect "as it was a best-selling machine anyway." One of the most spectacular cases of lack of effect was the Prestcold DP 101 dishwasher, rated a B.B. in the February 1963 issue of *Which?*—the model soon afterwards went out of production.

A market research survey (by Sales Research Services Ltd) carried out in August 1963 on factors influencing purchasers indicated that only 5 per cent specifically paid attention to *Which?* while another 5 per cent mentioned the B.B.C. programme "Choice", based on *Which?* reports. While consumers' replies to surveys of this kind are frequently at variance with their observed behaviour, as reflected in sales figures, and while the circulation of *Which?* has grown since that date, these findings support the view that only a minority are affected by test reports.

A rather more hopeful picture is presented if the circulation figures of the magazines in which the test results appear are examined. This approach also is subject to several difficulties of interpretation. In some countries more than one test magazine is published. For example, in the U.S.A. Consumer Research's *Consumer Bulletin* has a circulation of about 100,000, which should be added to the circulation figure for C.U.'s *Consumer Reports* in Table 1 below. More important, consumer test magazines vary considerably in the extent to which they stick to their last or go in for popular articles aimed at a wider audience (which latter kind of work also reduces the expense of production, for testing consumer durables is expensive). As mentioned, the Norwegian *Forbrukerraporten* was originally purely a test magazine but in 1960 changed over to a more popular type of publication (though without advertising) with test results relegated to a minor role. The paper received a grant of £100,000 from the government in 1960, but four years later had become self-supporting.

The pros and cons of these two types of publication raise many questions which need not concern us here. The experience of the U.K. Consumer Council's magazine *Focus*, launched in January 1966, which had only reached a circulation of 20,000 by 1968, suggests that a consumer magazine which *excludes* test reports is also likely to reach only a very small part of the population. Probably the best prospect is for a magazine mainly devoted to test results but containing a proportion of less technical material.

The circulation of the various test periodicals in 1962–64 is set out in Table 1. Increased circulation since that date should be borne in mind in interpreting the table. With three exceptions, Britain,

Canada, and the U.S.A., where 1964 figures are used, the figures relate to 1962 and 1963 and are taken from the International Organization of Consumers' Unions *Consumer Directory, 1964.* The circulation figure in Column (1) is divided by the population figure in Column (2) after the latter has been divided by four on the assumption that the average family consists of four people (the number of families rather than the number of individuals probably constitutes the possible upper limit for the circulation of a comparative test magazine).

TABLE 1

Circulation of consumer test magazines

	(1) Circulation	(2) Population (000)	(3) Circulation per 100 families
Canadian Consumer	18,000	18,200	0·40
Consumer Reports (U.S.A.)	880,000	187,000	1·72
Consumers' Tribune (Israel)	2,500	2,200	0·40
The Consumer (Japan)	30,000	96,500	0·12
Choice (Australia)	42,000	10,500	1·60
Consumer (New Zealand)	45,000	2,600	6·09
Konsument (Austria)	20,000	7,400	1·08
Test Achats (Belgium)	17,000	10,500	0·64
Rad og Resultater (Denmark)	16,000	4,800	1·33
Which? (U.K.)	416,000	54,900	3·08
Que Choisir (France)	2,000	46,900	0·01
Neytendabladid (Iceland)	8,000	180	17·78
Consumentengids (Netherlands)	55,000	12,000	1·80
Forbruker-raporten (Norway)	100,000	3,700	10·81
Rad och Ron (Sweden)	40,000	7,700	2·08

The results of these (inevitably very rough) calculations show that while test results may never reach more than a minority of the population, the size of the minority is much larger than is generally assumed. Assuming a readership of three consumer units (families or heads of households) per copy sold—by no means unreasonable, since a good number of subscribers must be libraries or other institutions, and it is known that many people rely on their friends for copies—it appears that in one country, Iceland, test results reach more than 50 per cent of the population, and in another, in Norway, they reach 30 per cent. On this calculation the commercial "D.M."

in Germany (not included in the table) would also reach 10 per cent, and this is only one of three magazines in Germany publishing comparative test results. In most other countries test results, at least in printed form, do not appear to reach more than 10 per cent of the population. But the figures for Iceland, Norway, and Germany indicate that the potential ceiling is very much higher.

On this analysis, the fact that there are few cases where test results have had any marked or sudden influence on sales is a matter for congratulation rather than otherwise—the explanation is presumably that the (more intelligent) sections of the community who subscribe to test publications make due allowance for their own individual needs and circumstances and do not merely pay regard to the "Best Buy". If this interpretation is correct one of the most frequent criticisms of comparative testing—that the "Best Buy" may be misleading if not read in conjunction with the other information in the test report, and suitably interpreted by consumers in the light of their individual requirements—appears to have little foundation.

3. *Criticisms of comparative testing*
The most frequent criticism of comparative testing concerns the practice of choosing a "Best Buy". As consumers' preferences differ, the *weighting* to be given to the various characteristics of a product in deciding on a "Best Buy" cannot accurately reflect the desires of all, or most, consumers. (A slightly different criticism, concerning the *subjectivity* of consumers' tastes, is mentioned later.) Consumer testing organizations, however, point out that the "Best Buy" procedure is quite a flexible one.[4] Also, provided the test results (and also if possible the test methods) are set out in full, so that the consumer can see what weighting has been adopted in arriving at a "Best Buy", there can be little serious objection. Quoting a "Best

[4] During 1964, for example, *Which?* gave no B.B. for eleven products tested (petrol, children's encyclopaedias, coffee-makers, stain removers, pork sausages, sanitary towels, cooking oils and fats, television-sets, cheap records, and ironing boards). More than one B.B. in each case was quoted for radiant convector heaters (4), twin tub washing machines (4), spin dryers, gas radiant convector heaters, electric fan heaters (3 B.B.s each), emulsion paints and distress signals for boats (2 B.B.s each). In contrast to these eighteen products for which no single B.B. was given, one Best Buy was quoted for ten products, prams (one each for high and low, with no B.B. for folding prams); power lawn mowers (one each for electric battery cylinder, electric mains cylinder, and petrol-driven mowers), boys' blazers, double-burning camping stoves, electric-drill attachments, language records, floor polishers, one-way nappies, medium-sized refrigerators, and electric fans.

Buy" on radio or television, where the full test results cannot be given (or, if they are, cannot be retained by the user of the information) is more open to criticism. So is the practice of quoting a "Best Buy" in a press summary of a test report, without the qualifications and criteria which may have been made clear in the full test report. However, these problems arise in all attempts to simplify and popularize rather complicated information. And, as noted, the fact that "Best Buys" have not in general had any marked or sudden impact on sales of the products named indicates that consumers who pay regard to test reports also take into account the necessary qualifications and their own requirements.

A more serious criticism is that the testing organization usually selects only one or a few samples of each of the brands to be tested. The Consumers' Association states that when one sample gives an "extreme" result, another is bought as a check. The simple answer to the criticism might be that if a consumer testing organization buying on the open market makes a purchase which is exceptionally poor or exceptionally good (of that brand) the ordinary consumer stands the same chance of doing so. Also, it could be argued that it is up to the manufacturer to improve his quality control so that "extreme" samples are as far as possible eliminated. These replies have substance, but do not altogether meet the point. Statistical theory indicates that a number of items have to be tested before an accurate picture of quality can be obtained. As far as the more expensive goods are concerned, this raises obvious difficulties for consumer testing organizations.

It may be possible to escape the dilemma by obtaining a consensus of opinion between the manufacturer and the testing organizations on whether the item tested is a fair sample of the product. *Which?* and most similar publications give the manufacturer the opportunity of commenting on the test results before they are published. However, if it is true that sub-standard items will continue to slip through the manufacturers' quality control net,[5] comparative testing will have to be supplemented by an efficient complaints system.

[5] Manufacturers frequently claim that the cost of quality control rises rapidly as it approaches 100 per cent—*i.e.*, that the cost of ensuring that only 1 or 2 out of every batch of 100 produced are deficient is much greater, *per unit of product*, than the cost of ensuring that only 9 or 10 out of every 100 are deficient. This might be supported by probability theory, but the author has not been able to find any empirical data to confirm it, despite inquiries of manufacturers and others. The absence of *economic* studies of quality control is again striking.

As consumer testing is still a fairly new art, mistakes may be made and test methods are likely to be progressively improved. International comparison of test methods is needed, as are studies of the methodology of testing, including a comparison of comparative test methods with the methods used by manufacturers for quality control. Manufacturers who feel aggrieved should also have the possibility of re-testing.

A more extreme criticism, which applies equally to comparative testing and labelling, is that as consumer choice is subjective, provision of objective information is useless or misleading. Although the source of this criticism is often suspect (business interests which might be adversely affected by consumer information), and it is sometimes stated in a rather naïve form—for example, that consumer information "takes all the fun out of shopping"—it deserves attention in view of the undeniable importance of subjective elements in consumer behaviour.

One aspect of the subjectivity of consumer choice has been mentioned, the fact that different consumers attach different degrees of importance to various characteristics of the product. It is therefore very difficult to give a "Best Buy" which is valid for all or the majority of consumers, but this is no argument against giving information on the separate quality characteristics of a product. Another aspect of the "subjectivity of choice" argument concerns the fact that for many products measurable characteristics are not the only ones, and perhaps not the most important ones, for the consumer.[6] In buying clothing, carpets, wallpaper, many items of furniture, and consumer durables, appearance is of considerable and often of decisive importance. However, this fact does not constitute an argument against providing information on measurable characteristics. Information about the durability and washability of carpets

[6] Confirmation of this point has come from the Communist countries recently. "It is the consumer's own subjective wants that weigh most with him, and he will gladly buy an item he likes even if it should, for example, be second class. . . . Every salesman engaged in the distributive trades will confirm that the first thing a consumer considers is whether a piece of cloth appeals to the eye, what it feels like to touch, and to grip it, whether a suit fits, whether a shoe is comfortable and so on. He will be much less concerned with small faults in the weave or small scratches on the leather." (J. Kornai, *Overcentralisation in Economic Administration.*) On the other hand, it might be that consumers in the Soviet countries have suffered a shortage of consumer goods that are both stylish and of high performance quality, and it may be that, as in the West, there is a lack of information on testable quality characteristics.

and wallpaper does not prevent the consumer taking into account both his individual preference as regards style and colour, or giving his preference as regards style and colour whatever importance he wishes to attach to it in comparison with the importance he wishes to assign to durability and washability. Indeed, if the consumer has no information available on objective factors (as is usually the case in the absence of comparative testing and labelling) he cannot rationally decide what relative importance he is to attach to, for example, appearance and durability, and is forced to decide exclusively on the basis of the former.

Finally, some of the criticisms which have been made of comparative testing are more a reflection on manufacturers. As the U.S. Consumers' Union points out in the monthly preface to its *Consumer Reports*, "So long as quality varies within brands and products change within their names, no test results can give infallible guidance."

4. *Labelling*

In one sense labels—brand names, the name of the manufacturer or place of origin, directions for use of varying degrees of helpfulness, or labels carrying advertisements for the product—are almost universal and have been so since pre-packaging became widespread in the latter part of the nineteenth century. Our concern here is with labelling of performance characteristics, preferably in a number of grades on a scale such as 1 to 5 or 1 to 10. Labelling in this sense was almost unknown in Britain until the Consumer Council introduced its Teltag labels in 1967. In most other countries except Holland and Sweden informative labelling is also notable by its absence, except for products such as food and medicines, where the reason for it lies in health and safety rather than in enabling the consumer to make a rational economic choice.

For the simplest products—matches, cigarettes, many foodstuffs—the consumer needs to know little except the quantity or number of items. With other products such as detergents or household cleansers, the main thing needed on a label is the quantity of *effective* product, defined according to a standard unit of cleaning power. This is now technically feasible (see the U.S. Consumers' Union *Consumer Reports*, August 1967, page 426). Labelling with effective cleaning power was proposed in the earlier drafts of the "Truth-in-Packaging" Act, which became law in the U.S. in July 1966, but was dropped after objections by trade interests. The U.S. Act, and legislation which came into force in Britain in 1965 (the Weights and Measures Act, 1963), made it obligatory to state number or quantity for most products where this is feasible and desirable.

The kind of information needed on more complex products is indicated by comparative test reports and from British Standards Institution specifications. To take a few examples from reports in *Which?*:

Suitcases. Tests were devised to measure resistance to stubbing (with a sharp point), squashing, bumping, and scuffing; handle strength; carrying comfort; permeability to rain; and stability. Performance on all these qualities was graded from 1 to 4. In addition the test reports contained information on size, weight, locks, and hinges. *Stair carpets*: two characteristics were tested and graded: surface loss, and loss of appearance. In principle it is desirable to compare the results of these kinds of laboratory and mechanical tests with *performance in use*, but the latter might take several years. Other products might taken even longer—for example a twenty-year period might be needed to test the performance in use of clocks. In such cases mechanical tests may not correlate exactly with performance in use, but provided it is not attempted to define and measure a large number of grades the difference should not generally be important. *Twin-tub washing machines* were tested for washing efficiency, rinsing efficiency, spin-drying efficiency, absence of creasing, and time taken for washing, rinsing, and spin drying. The test results also contained information on the cost per lb. of washing; running costs; and ease of use (*e.g.*, if the machine contained a timer, thermostat, or heater cut-out; and whether it was noisy, or difficult to load).

With the most complex products such as cars the number of characteristics on which information is needed may run into hundreds.

In testing textile products, the performance characteristics are evident from specifications used by the British Standards Institution and similar standards organizations. Standard tests exist for resistance to heat, light, water, and abrasion. Labels should also contain information on materials used in construction (wool/cotton/synthetic fibres in textiles, leather or synthetic materials in shoes, wood/plastics in furniture) to enable consumers who have preferences as regards material to satisfy them, especially in buying textile products.[7] However, labelling by materials alone may be the

[7] Consumers may also need to know the textile material used for washing, etc.

reverse of helpful, owing to a widespread but quite fallacious belief among consumers that traditional materials such as wool and leather are inherently superior to synthetic materials. Pressure for materials labelling has come mainly from producers of traditional materials. The U.S. Wool Products Labelling Act of 1939 and Textile Fibres Identification Act of 1960 were introduced mainly in response to this kind of pressure. It is true that synthetic materials when first introduced for clothing, footwear, and other consumer goods were often inferior to their traditional counterparts, but synthetics have undergone a process of continuous improvement; and if a difference still exists it would be adequately indicated by performance labelling.

Another danger is that labelling schemes adopted on a purely national basis, especially when obligatory, may have a protectionist motivation, and it is therefore urgent to obtain internationally agreed labelling schemes.

A distinction is sometimes drawn between "informative labelling" and "quality labelling", the former being used to describe labels such as the Consumer Council's Teltag and the latter to describe labels like the Kite Mark of the British Standards Institution. The Kite Mark is awarded to products (mainly bedding and furniture) which comply with minimum specifications laid down by the B.S.I. It is now widely agreed that the latter type is of limited value. Except where health and safety considerations are involved (*e.g.*, fire extinguishers, life-belts) a simple classification into "Pass" or "Fail" categories is of much less use to the consumer than several grades; and where health and safety considerations are involved substandard products should be illegal.[8]

There are really only two important questions in a labelling scheme. One is the technical one of specifications and testing methods. As indicated above, this is not a compelling problem; the comparative testing organizations are doing the basic research which is needed for deciding the content of labels. The British Standards Institution has had for many years standard methods of test for some 200 consumer goods, though until recently these were not mainly concerned with evolving graded performance characteristics. The second problem is the acceptance or coverage of labels—*i.e.*, what percentage of goods sold in a particular product line carry

---

[8] It is illegal in Britain to sell motor-cyclists' crash helmets, or rear lamps and reflectors on vehicles, which do not comply with the relevant British Standard. Electric blankets, oil heaters, and car safety belts also usually carry the B.S.I. Kite Mark.

H

labels. Neither the British Standards Institution as regards its Kite Mark scheme nor the Consumer Council for its Teltags is able to give any information on the market coverage of their respective schemes (another indication of the absence of economists in consumer protection bodies!). But it is clear that Kite Marks never covered a large part of the market even in furniture and bedding. At the time of writing, the Teltag is still in its early stages.

5. *Political representation of consumers*

The first modern peace-time organizations for representation of consumers in government were those set up in the U.S.A. under the National Industrial Recovery Act and the Agricultural Adjustment Act of 1933. The first Act introduced industrial codes largely designed to prevent price cutting. The latter aimed at "stabilization" of agricultural prices by means of production control. Both consumer bodies had an inauspicious existence. Since the programmes under which they were established were basically anti-consumer, they could only deal with such questions as whether a given retail price increase was justified on the basis of specified increases in agricultural or manufacturing prices. Thus the Consumer Council of the Agricultural Adjustment Administration found itself considering what was the fair retail price for a cotton shirt, taking into account both the A.A.A. and the N.I.R.A. programmes. It is not surprising that in the outcome "the New Deal consumer organizations had little influence on the course of events."[9]

As mentioned in the preceding chapter, provision for equal representation of consuming *countries* was made in the commodity control schemes set up under United Nations auspices since the Second World War. However, the effective restraint on price increases has come from the bargaining power of consuming countries,

[9] Persia Campbell, *Consumer Representation in the New Deal* (Columbia University Press, 1940), p. 262. Professor Campbell believes that this lack of influence "was due not to the unreality of the consumer interest, nor its want of significance in promoting the general welfare, but to the lack of bargaining strength in the total consumer position. The main problem that presents itself therefore is how to bring the consumer interest effectively to bear in the functioning of the national economy as a whole, and particularly in the formulation and administration of public policy towards industry (including agriculture)." The Chairman of the meetings between consumer and producer representatives, a retired general, was given to discomfiting the former by shouting at them "Who is the consumer? Show me a consumer!" (*op. cit.*, p. 31.)

which will of course exist with or without formal consumer representation; the likelihood of substitution of other materials if prices rise; and pressure by low-cost producers within the agreement for a larger share of the market (as well as pressure by producers outside the agreement).

To represent consumers *vis-à-vis* the Common Market institutions a Consumers's Contact Committee was set up in Brussels in April 1962, comprising four kinds of organization: consumers' organizations in the six member countries of the E.E.C. (including the Bureau Européen des Unions de Consommateurs), trade unions, women's organizations, and national co-operatives. The Contact Committee is represented on the Consultative Committees set up by the Common Market Commission for products regulated by the Common Agricultural Policy. The Committee seems to be doing useful work on such matters as harmonization of national food regulations on permitted additives but appears so far to have had a negligible effect on decisions on prices and levies. The price decisions have been based on the needs of the different producer groups within the E.E.C. and—to some extent—the claims of outside producers such as Denmark and the U.S.A. for a share of the E.E.C. market. While it is impossible to prove that in the absence of consumer representation prices might not have been fixed even higher, the development of the Common Agricultural Policy has so far been determinedly protectionist.[10]

Of the National Industrial Recovery Administration the international commodity agreements and the Common Market agricultural consultative committees it might be said that these are explicitly produced-orientated bodies and that consumer representation on them was doomed to ineffectiveness from the outset. The

[10] "The Commission has accepted consumer representation in the consultative committees. But only certain technical questions concerning the application of market rules (can be) considered. . . . Consumers bitterly regret that they are unable to take part in discussions except at a stage when work is far advanced. . . . In reality, the situation is as follows: the Commission deliberates at first, within the framework of the basic rules and in considering the statistics with producers; it then fixes the regulations in such a way that afterwards there is nothing left to modify. It is not rare for consumers to learn of the existence of proposals by the Commission only after these have been submitted to the Council, or even accepted." Dr A. Schone, European Union of Consumer Co-operative Central Production and Wholesale Societies, quoted in the International Co-operative Alliance's *Consumer Affairs Bulletin*, No. 5, 1963.

question arises whether organizations set up to promote the consumer interest in a wider sphere, such as the Consumer Advisory Council in the U.S.A. and the Consumer Council in Britain, can play a more useful role. These may be referred to as "umbrella" organizations since their task is to take an overall view of the consumer interest, assess the effectiveness of other organizations working in this field, and take action to remedy any evident gaps.

The U.S. Consumer Advisory Council was established in July 1962 following President Kennedy's Message to Congress on "Measures for protecting the consumer interest" in March 1962. The C.A.C. was given no specific terms of reference but in September 1962 it declared that it would devote its attention to ten subjects of pressing interest to consumers: consumer standards, grades, and labels; improvement of the two-way flow of information and opinion between government and the consumer; effective consumer representation in government; consumer credit; the inter-relation among Federal and State agencies in consumer protection; acceleration of economic growth; improvement of levels of consumption of low-income groups; anti-trust action and prevention of price-fixing; adequate housing; and medical care.

Some changes were made in January 1964, with the aim of giving consumer representatives more direct access to the President. A Special Assistant on Consumer Affairs (Mrs Esther Peterson) was appointed and a President's Committee on Consumer Interests was established to which the Consumer Advisory Council, which had previously functioned as part of the President's Council of Economic Advisors, was now to be subordinated. The Committee on Consumer Interests was to advise the government on issues of broad economic policy affecting consumers; on government action to meet consumer needs; and on improvements in the flow of consumer research material to the public. This Committee, President Johnson said, would "ensure that the voice of the consumer would be loud, clear, uncompromising and effective in the highest councils of Federal government. . . . For the first time in history, the American consumer's interest—so closely identified with the public interest— will be directly represented in the White House. . . . The Committee will be vigilant to keep consumers informed so that they are not completely at the mercy of those who exact unfair prices or levy unfair charges."

In Britain, a government-financed Consumer Council was set up in May 1963 following the Final Report of the Molony Committee on Consumer Protection. The Molony Committee was established in 1959 as a result of rapidly-growing interest in consumer matters, including the success of *Which?* Proposals for a national Consumer Council had figured in many discussions of consumer questions in the early 1950's, but most of these were concerned with the absence of a comparative testing organization and assumed that a Consumer Council would include this among its major functions. Others saw in it a means of gathering together under one roof the consumer protection functions at present scattered about among different government departments, the Board of Trade dealing with hire-purchase legislation and misleading advertising, the Home Office with safety matters in consumer goods, the Ministry of Agriculture with food labelling, additives, and related questions; and the Ministry of Health with safety of medicines.

The Molony Committee argued that comparative testing was already being done efficiently by a private organization (though it had some reservations about the "oligarchic constitution" of the Consumers' Association) and that it was not the function of a government-sponsored organization to discriminate between the products of different manufacturers (para. 851). Therefore the new Consumer Council should not undertake comparative testing. Individual consumer complaints were also excluded from the Council's province because of the expense. The Committee quoted the estimate of the Consumer Advisory Council of the British Standards Institution that complaints cost on average £4 or £5 each to deal with. Also, a free complaints service was likely to lead to an increase in the number of unjustified complaints. Finally, law enforcement action was excluded. Thus, the work which the Council was not to do was clearly set out, but the guidance on what it *should* do was rather vague. "The basic concern of the Council would be to inform itself about, and to keep under review, the problems experienced by the consumer, and to devise and advance the means of solving them" (para. 850).

There have been considerable advances in legislative protection for consumers both in Britain and in the U.S.A. since the state-sponsored consumer protection organizations came into being (the Hire Purchase Act, 1964, and the Trade Descriptions Act of 1968 in Britain, and the Truth-in-Packaging and Truth-in-Lending Acts in the U.S.A.). But there is no cause-and-effect relationship as the legislation in question was under way before the two organizations were set up, and it is not clear that they have accelerated it.

Both can claim a number of successes. The Consumer Council in Britain has taken up a number of kinds of deceptive sales practices and exposed them in its monthly magazine *Focus*. The American body was instrumental in the Defence Department's direction that fair contracts and full disclosure of interest charges should be adopted in dealings with members of the armed forces, and has urged State governments to improve their consumer fraud statutes. Both organizations have done much to promote consumer education in schools, and have played a part in international consumer organizations.

If the prevailing feeling is one of disappointment at what state-sponsored consumer "umbrella" organizations have achieved to date there seems to be two main explanations. One is the lack of specific terms of reference, and in the case of the American organization topics were included in its remit, such as the acceleration of economic growth and reform of taxation, which could not by any stretch of imagination be appropriately included in the ambit of a consumer organization. Secondly, both organizations lack a research capability. It is arguable that government organizations of this kind cannot successfully innovate, and that innovation must be the prime task of a consumer organization. It is difficult to imagine any government body producing, for example, a report like Mr Ralph Nader's book *Unsafe at any Speed* which has revolutionized safety standards in the car industry not only in the U.S.A. but all over the world. But if an organization of this kind is to make a serious contribution it must possess economic, social, and technical research expertise of a high order. More specific terms of reference might also help. Their main spheres should probably be consumer education (particularly in schools) and consumer research. The attempt to take on any and every subject affecting consumer welfare is probably futile.

Finally, it might have been expected that the mere establishment of government consumer councils would not in itself lead to many significant advances in the position of the consumer, and it is not unfair to say that among the motives for their establishment was the desire of politicians to "cash in" on the widespread feeling that they should do, and should be seen to be doing, something to help consumers. However, as our analysis of pressure groups indicated, the establishment of a representative organization is neither necessary nor sufficient for improving the economic position of those represented.

6. *Some problems and conclusions*
Labelling and comparative testing
The main advantages of labelling over testing are that it is immediately and continuously available at the point of sale; quality changes are shown immediately on the label, while comparative testing of a particular product takes place only at intervals; it is fairly inexpensive and its cost is borne by the producer; and it is easier for the consumer to absorb the limited and simplified information given. The last point indicates the prime disadvantage of labelling—the number of characteristics about which information can be given is limited, and it cannot take into account variations *within* quality grades. The number of characteristics which can be described is small (at least on labels as conventionally conceived—no doubt a booklet attached to a product might be described as a label). Even more important, the buyer will not know, unless they are on display at the point of sale, whether there are other brands which might meet his requirements better.

For these reasons labelling is unlikely to provide a complete substitute for testing for the more expensive and complex consumer durables such as cars, television- and radio-sets, washing machines, refrigerators, sewing machines, watches, and cameras, though for other products labelling alone may be sufficient. However, the two forms of information need not be regarded as substitutes. As the demand for consumer information grows, very likely both will continue to grow simultaneously, and it does not seem that in most countries comparative test organizations have reached the ceiling of their potential circulation.

Voluntary and compulsory labelling
A voluntary labelling scheme has to be supported by considerable publicity if it is to be accepted. The Consumer Council's Teltag scheme, originally due to come into force in 1965, did not really get off the ground until 1968.[11] What coverage—both as regards the number of products, and the market shares of individual products—can be achieved with this kind of voluntary scheme has yet to be

[11] The Council's Director, writing in *The Sunday Times* (August 28th, 1966, p. 11) in reply to a criticism that the Teltag scheme was taking a long time to get started, said that "The preliminary work, with the fullest co-operation from manufacturers, has taken longer than expected (two years—in Sweden it took seven) but this does not affect the chances of success once the labels are in the shops."

seen. The first products carrying Teltags were electric kettles, and a variety of food-preparation machines and attachments—kneaders, blenders, mincers, shredders, slicers, juice extractors, potato-peelers, sieves, coffee-grinders, and coffee-mills. The first Teltags for textiles, for non-washable floor rugs, were also introduced in 1968.

But there seems no strong reason why a labelling scheme, once the need for it and the test methods are agreed, should not be made obligatory. This possibility has been little discussed, mainly because the need for labelling has been seen mainly in a "health and safety" context and the economic reasons for it have been underestimated, although the Molony Committee did suggest obligatory care-labelling of textiles. If labelling were compulsory, not only would the lengthy and expensive process of publicity and education for a voluntary scheme be eliminated. So also would the need for a permanent organization to grant, supervise, and promote labels. (The technical test methods would as at present be drawn up by the British Standards Institution or the Consumers' Association, or by both jointly.)

The Molony Committee, in its discussions of the Merchandise Marks Acts, stated (para. 655): "We recommend that *power be taken* to prohibit consumer trade in designated goods unless they bear a label or are accompanied on delivery with a written statement conveying prescribed information. . . ." (our italics). But the Committee gave no indication of what goods should be dealt with under these powers, beyond saying that goods for which the power already exists, such as food and drugs, seeds, fertilizers, and pharmaceutical products, should be excluded. In fact, the only criterion for introducing obligatory labelling should be that there is a need for it, and that methods of test have been agreed.

The cost of consumer information
The economist automatically thinks of the benefits of consumer information in relation to its costs, while consumer organizations have simply stressed the desirability of providing it. To a large extent, of course, consumer information must itself be regarded as a means of reducing the cost of shopping. A typical comparative test report contains information on twenty to forty brands. The consumer would be unlikely to find all these in one shop, and would have to devote a considerable amount of time and energy to examining them physically, even if qualified to do so. However, because of the absence of a cost approach to information provision, trade interests

who wish to damage the cause of consumer information and more rational shopping have been able to point to the absurdity of, for example, expecting the shopper to spend 3*d.* on a bus fare to save 1*d.* in price.

Labelling may be considerably superior to comparative testing on the score of costs, not only in that the individual consumer pays nothing (or very little) for the label, but labels if generally adopted reach all or most potential buyers. Once a labelling scheme is generally adopted the cost to the producer is very small per unit of product sold. It may be possible to make comparative test reports more easily and cheaply available. *Which?* is normally filed in public libraries, and files might also be held in retail outlets (especially department stores and non-food co-operative shops) where the retailer might provide them free, or the prospective buyer could examine them for a small fee. Such a scheme would probably be unwelcome to the comparative test organizations, as their revenue would not increase as much as if consumers continued to subscribe individually, but it should be possible to meet this problem by payments by the store to the comparative testing organization or by State subsidies.

While it is foolish to suppose that progress can be made without considerable effort on the part of consumers themselves to secure value for money, all possible means should be explored of making consumer information more accessible as well as extending the volume of information available. The problem is part of the more general "information explosion". If they wish to make wise choices people have to absorb an increasing amount of information not only as purchasers of goods and services but also on matters such as work, the social services, investment, the use of leisure, and what may be broadly described as questions of citizenship. In the long run, the problem may be solved by improved storage and retrieval systems for information—it has been suggested that television and telephone systems may enable the consumer to do most of his shopping, if he wishes, without leaving home, and computer-telephone links may enable him to compare prices as well as value for money. In the meantime a study of the costs and effectiveness of the different methods of providing information (comparative testing, labelling, or pre-purchase advice centres[12]) would be of considerable use.

[12] On the state-subsidized consumer clinic in Vienna, see *The Times*, October 4th, 1966.

The seller's responsibility

As far as possible the cost of providing adequate information about the product he sells should be borne by the seller—the manufacturer or retailer. This consideration again gives labelling an important advantage compared with comparative testing. However, while manufacturers could be legally obliged to provide information by means of labels, it is difficult to see any single or easy solution at the retail level other than through a lead from the more progressive retailers.

The principle that the cost should be borne by the seller—in this case the trade association rather than the manufacturer or retailer—is applicable to complaints, if only to give sellers an incentive to reduce the number of complaints by quality control and pre-purchase information. Many trade associations already run schemes for arbitrating consumer complaints. Among the best known in Britain are those of the National House-Builders' Registration Council, the Motor Agents' Association, and the Association of British Travel Agents. In each case, of course, the arbitration scheme extends only to traders who are members. The Better Business Bureaux in the U.S.A. operate similar schemes on a multi-trade basis. These schemes may not be perfect—some of them contain clauses preventing, or trying to prevent, the consumer from exercising his normal legal rights if he disagrees with the findings of the arbitrator. However, in many cases they provide the only effective channel for complaints. A consumer wishing to go to law would probably have to obtain a technical test, costing £2 to £5 at least (the normal minimum charge of testing organizations) in addition to the expense and time involved in the legal process, which would be highly irrational behaviour for any product costing less than this sum. Provided they operate under suitable rules to guarantee fairness, there is no reason why trade organizations should not work satisfactorily as arbitrators.

At present consumer complaints in Britain are officially dealt with by the Citizens' Advice Bureaux. C.A.B. are staffed by voluntary workers and deal with a wide range of problems besides "consumer" problems. The Consumer Council, as recommended by the Molony Committee, is prohibited by its terms of reference from taking up individual complaints, and relies largely on the C.A.B. for information about complaints. The arrangement seems to have led to some friction between the two bodies, and the Director of the Consumer Council, writing in the Council's magazine *Focus*, for May 1967, suggested a national chain of local offices under the Council's aegis to deal with complaints. However, the fundamental question is not who deals with complaints, but whether subsidized test facilities should be made available to complainants. The reason the C.A.B. have not been able to deal with complaints to the complainant's satisfaction has usually been because technical tests are needed and the C.A.B. are unable either to undertake, or to help finance, testing. The Consumer Council's Director remarked in the same article "I do not believe that the volume of valid consumer complaints (although too large) is large enough to justify a testing service at the public expense." A local complaints office of the Consumer Council which could not help consumers with testing would find itself in essentially the same difficulty in dealing with consumer complaints as the Citizens' Advice Bureaux have done.

8

Consumer Representation in Nationalized Industry

As the users of underground and suburban railways know to their cost, certain Railway Companies habitually sell non-existent places in third-class carriages, and if, much against his will, the unfortunate traveller enters a carriage of another class, proceed to collect from him the excess fare to which the inadequacy of their arrangements have made him liable. If the railways were nationalized the Press would ring with protests against State incompetence and the sharp practice of officials. Since they are in private hands, not a murmur is heard. . . . the view commonly expressed by the business world, that a public service is likely to ride roughshod over the consumer, appears to be the precise opposite of the truth.

R. H. TAWNEY[1]

On the one hand, the public corporation does not at present appear to be satisfactorily accountable to anyone. Parliament exercises only a fitful power of debate (usually long after the event); the Minister exerts some unknown degree of control behind the scenes; while the corporations are less sensitive than their private counterparts to the normal pressures of the profit motive and the price mechanism.

C. A. R. CROSLAND[2]

1. Why nationalization?

Not many generalizations about the motives, necessity, or justification of nationalization stand up to examination in the light of historical experience in different countries. In Britain, probably the main reason for nationalization was the belief that certain industries, especially gas, electricity, telephones, and the railways, are "natural

---

[1] *The Acquisitive Society* (G. Bell and Sons, London, 1930), pp. 145–146.
[2] "The private and public corporation in Great Britain", in E. S. Mason (ed.), *The Corporation in Modern Society* (Harvard University Press, 1960), p. 274.

monopolies" owing to the scale of capital investment required and the nature of the distributive network. In the decision to nationalize the coal industry and the railways, an important factor was the belief that there was inadequate investment and low efficiency of operation in the pre-war period when the industries were in private hands, but other industries, such as ship-building, which might also be charged with inefficiency remained in private hands.

In other countries examples, many successful, are to be found of such "natural monopolies" being run by private enterprise, usually with some degree of public supervision. In the U.S.A. the privately owned telephone system has reached a high pitch of efficiency, in strong contrast to the publicly owned postal service. Most electricity undertakings in the U.S.A. are privately owned, and some notably successful consumer co-operatives operate in this field.

Labour Party members often say that "basic" or "essential" industries should be in public ownership. However, from the consumer's standpoint the most essential industries are food, fuel, housing, clothing, and medical services. The Labour Party's definition often implies that "heavy" industries (another highly ambiguous term, which seems to mean roughly the same as "capital goods" industries) are more essential than others. This, like the belief that investment in capital goods industries is more essential for a country's economic development than investment in consumer goods industries or in services, has no rational foundation. Substitutes can be, and have been, found for coal, iron and steel, railways, cement, and other capital goods industries.

If the problem is seen as carrying out specific objectives of government policy, such as preventing unemployment, controlling inflation, accelerating the rate of economic growth, or mitigating inequality in the ownership of capital and incomes, it is by no means clear that nationalization is necessary for the achievement of these objectives, or that it is a more efficient means to these ends than alternative means. The battery of fiscal, monetary, and physical controls at the disposal of the government may be more effective. Many (perhaps most) members of the Labour Party in Britain would accept this argument, which was propagated by Mr Gaitskell (whose article "The economic aims of the Labour Party" in the *Political Quarterly*, January–March 1953, is one of its earliest statements) and by Mr C. A. R. Crosland,[3] now President of the Board of Trade.

[3] Especially in *The Future of Socialism* (Jonathan Cape, London, 1956).

In any case, it is generally not in the interests of the nation, the consumer or the industry concerned that a particular industry should be called upon to bear the cost of national policies. If, for example, it is desired to prevent depopulation of the North of Scotland, the electricity and railway industries should not be called upon to provide subsidies to the region out of their own revenues. To do so would raise the cost of their services in other parts of the country and make them less able to compete. An example of the consequences of internal subsidization in the coal industry is that some electricity generating stations in the East Midlands coalfield area (the most efficient in Britain) use oil rather than coal. The price of coal sold by the East Midland pits was kept high in order to subsidize other, less efficient, coal-mining areas.

Nor do the generalizations which at one time were current, for example, on the unsuitability of nationalized industries to risk-bearing and innovation, amount to much in the light of recent history. We need only mention the Italian oil and natural gas enterprises, the Irish Sugar Company, and the Renault and Volkswagen car firms (both the latter were nationalized for purely fortuitous reasons). Apart from railways and air transport, which are nationalized in most countries, international comparisons do not yield any firm conclusions as to which industries are most suitable for nationalization. In Britain the nationalized industries are coal, gas, electricity, the railways, the major airlines, and most of the steel industry (plus the Atomic Energy Commission, the B.B.C., the Post Office, and the Bank of England, all of which are outside the scope of the present discussion), while in France the main nationalized industries are chemicals, motor vehicles, aircraft, cigarettes, and matches; in West Germany, they include shipyards; in the Netherlands, the mining industry; and so on.

We do not here attempt to pronounce on the right criteria for nationalization, but merely note that the question raises a number of difficulties.

Among earlier advocates of nationalization in Britain, some hoped for a syndicalist solution with various forms of workers' control. This line of thinking was influential in the early years of the twentieth century and again in the 1920's. It became of less importance after the Labour Government of 1929–31, when Mr Herbert Morrison (then Minister of Transport) decided that the members of the management board of a public corporation should be appointed on grounds of ability alone, and that the decision on whom to appoint should rest solely with the Minister concerned. The principle was embodied in the then newly formed London Passenger Transport Board. Syndicalism, if workable, would have been unfortunate in the industries which were later nationalized in Britain, as they were in most cases given a monopoly of their productive sector. (More accurately, they have a higher degree of monopoly than most private firms.) There is, of course, no valid argument against workers' representation or participation on the boards of nationalized industries, which may be essential for effective communication between management and workers. The objection is only to a situation in which all, or a majority of, the board is elected by workers in the industry concerned.

2. Consumer representation in the British nationalized industries

In all the industries nationalized in 1945–51, provision was made for representation of consumers. For the coal industry, two consumers' organizations were set up at the national level, the Industrial Coal Consumers' Council and the Domestic Coal Consumers' Council, with the duties of considering any matter "affecting the supply of coal, coke or manufactured fuel" which is the subject of representations to them by consumers, or is referred to them by the Minister of Power. The Minister may give directives to the Board on the basis of recommendations made by the Consumers' Councils, but he has not in fact done so (in the early post-war period, he occasionally put pressure on the National Coal Board not to raise prices, even though the N.C.B.'s case for raising them had been accepted by the Consumers' Councils).

The annual reports of the two coal Consumers' Councils are generally brief documents, part of which is taken up with a summary of the annual report of the National Coal Board for the same year. Both Councils have expressed concern about the upward trend of prices, the Industrial Council sometimes adding its view that industrial consumers are being unfairly treated and the Domestic Council that domestic users are being discriminated against. In addition the Industrial Council has concerned itself with such matters as regional differences in prices, summer-winter price differentials, and the need for better rail and port facilities for the transport of coal. The Domestic Council was able to induce the N.C.B. and other organizations to take action on the availability of smokeless fuels in areas which were being brought under the Clean Air Act, the availability of pre-packed fuels, and moisture in coke. It has also given publicity to allegedly excessive prices charged by private dealers for pre-packed coal and has influenced the private coal retail trade by encouraging the extension of the Approved Coal Merchants' Scheme.[4] The Domestic Consumers' Council, while willing to accept complaints from individual consumers, can usually only inform complainants that their legal redress is against the merchant from whom they bought their coal, not against the N.C.B.

In the gas and electricity industries, unlike the coal industry, the consumers' organizations are on a regional basis. For each of the fourteen Area Electricity Boards, and each of the twelve Area Gas Boards, the Minister of Power must appoint a Consultative Council. Electricity Consultative Councils deal with such questions as the accuracy of meter readings (especially the Area Boards' practice of estimating the reading when the meter reader is unable to obtain access to the premises); payment of electricity accounts in easy stages; the cost of connection to the electricity supply. The complexities of electricity tariffs give rise to ample scope for misunderstanding (most, though not all, on the part of consumers) and in both gas and electricity the introduction of mechanized accounting systems has given rise to problems which the Consultative Councils have to explain.

The electricity Consultative Councils also receive inquiries and complaints about the safety of domestic electrical appliances. They have to explain that the Electricity Boards do not ensure that the work of a private contractor carrying out an installation is up to standard before providing a supply of electricity, as they cannot carry out a full inspection, and merely see that the work is not obviously faulty. The Board, or the Consultative Council, will advise consumers to see that the contractor doing the work is on the approved list of the National Inspection Council for Electrical Installation Contracting (N.I.C.E.I.C.).

Subjects on which the gas Consultative Councils receive complaints include delay in supply by Gas Boards of spare parts for appliances, disputed accounts, inadequate gas pressure, re-instate-

---

[4] An Approved Coal Merchant undertakes to supply solid fuels throughout the year, to stock a wide range of fuels, to show the N.C.B. group number or designation of house coal on all delivery notes and advertisements, and "to investigate promptly and sympathetically all complaints by consumers regarding fuel or service, and, where these appear justified, to make adequate and speedy redress". If a complaint is not met by the merchant, a consumer can ask a regional panel set up under the Approved Coal Merchants' Scheme to arbitrate.

ment of roads after laying of mains, and unsatisfactory fitting of appliances.

Under the Transport Acts of 1947 and 1962 there are eleven Area Transport Users' Consultative Committees and a Central Transport Consultative Committee. The Committees consider complaints about railway passengers, closures and the standard of rail services, including over-crowding, punctuality of trains, station car parks, and train meals. As there is a specialist body, the Transport Tribunal, to supervise the fares of public transport authorities, the Transport Consultative Committees have regarded fares as outside the scope of their work.

Since about 1960 they have been heavily occupied with the railways' programme of reducing uneconomic services, and have scored some successes on questions such as the deletion of certain services from train time-tables before their abandonment had been agreed. In 1961, when this question was raised, the British Transport Commission "pointed out reasonably enough that months must elapse between a time-table going into press and its coming into force. What might appear to be 'jumping the gun' was, they maintain, no more than an attempt to estimate what they hoped would be the position when the new time-table came into operation. But they now accept that less criticism would be forthcoming if the suspended services were maintained in the time-table, and their withdrawal during the currency of a time-table ... announced in the first available supplement."[5] Despite this, two years later the Central Consultative Committee said that it had noticed cases where the reduction of cheap-ticket facilities and deletion of services from time-tables had taken place on lines which were still being considered for closure. "There may be operational reasons for doing this kind of thing, but the effect on the Board's public relations is bad."[6]

The Transport Tribunals have their origin in the Railway and Canal Commission Act of 1888. The Transport Act of 1947 created a Railway Transport Tribunal to which the newly formed British Transport Commission had to submit proposed modifications in its charges. The procedure involved giving notice, hearing objections, and a public inquiry, after which the Tribunal could confirm, amend,

[5] Report of the Central Transport Consultative Committee for the year ended 31st December, 1961.

[6] Report of the Central Transport Consultative Committee for the year ended 31st December, 1963.

or reject the B.T.C.'s proposals. Since 1953 the powers of the Transport Tribunal have been greatly reduced, and it now determines maximum charges only for the carriage of freight by rail, and maximum passenger charges in the London area. This reflects the change in the economic position of the railways from a high degree of monopoly to a service subject to increasing competition from road transport.

3. *The verdict on consumer representation*
In 1948, Mr Morrison said:

> I want the consumers' councils to be powerful and to insist on having the facts to judge specific cases. I want them to be critically-minded in every good sense of the term and I want their reports to the Ministers and the public to be frank. They must be ready to fight when it is necessary for them to fight. These bodies can become important if they are properly run and the consumers' representatives are sufficiently active and vigorous.

However, the verdict of most studies of the councils has been adverse. Several studies have shown that only a small minority of the population is aware of their existence. "There is general agreement among a considerable number of investigators and competent observers that the councils have fulfilled their purpose to a limited extent, but that in general the results so far have been less far-reaching than might have been expected."[7]

In 1956 an official committee of inquiry into the electricity industry concluded:

> There is little doubt in our opinion that the vast majority of electricity consumers throughout the country are completely ignorant of the existence or purpose of the [electricity consultative] councils. We are nevertheless satisfied that in a quiet and modest way the councils have done and are doing creditable work in safeguarding the consumer's interest. The value and quality of their work varies from area to area, but we are left with the impression that the general body of consumers are well served by their councils. The effectiveness of the consultative councils should not merely be measured by reference to the number of grievances about which consumers have felt concerned enough to bring them to the attention of the councils. In our view the very existence of the councils has served as a constant check on the Area Boards,

[7] W. A. Robson, *Nationalized Industry and Public Ownership* (Allen and Unwin, 2nd edition, 1962), p. 237.

who are obliged under the Act to consult with the councils about their general policies and arrangements.[8]

If it is true that the great majority of electricity consumers are ignorant of the existence or purpose of the Consultative Councils the view that they have nevertheless done useful work would seem to require considerable justification, which is not provided in the committee's report. A more critical judgment on the councils is that of Political and Economic Planning:

> These bodies have few powers and are of little use. Their weakness lies as much in their terms of reference as in their composition. Meeting rarely, run on civil service lines, with no research staff of their own, with disinterested consumers in the minority and with little finance to draw attention to their existence, they are very imperfect representatives of consumers. Their annual reports make pathetic reading.[9]

Several critics have pointed out that a Consultative Council whose staff is dependent on the producer Board for wages, accommodation, and information is not likely to be very critical of the Board. This could be remedied comparatively easily. Already the Ministry of Power, not the National Coal Board, meets the expenses of the Industrial and Domestic Coal Consumers' Councils, and since the Electricity Act of 1957 the Electricity Council, not the Area Boards, pays the expenses of the electricity Consultative Councils.

An increase in staff—at present a secretary (sometimes part-time) with one or two clerks and shorthand typists—is evidently necessary. Professor Robson has pointed out that "Not one of the Councils is in a position to undertake an inquiry involving a knowledge of economics, statistics, accountancy or any branch of engineering. . . . Without such personnel they will always have to accept what factual or other information the public corporation chooses to give them." In discussing consumer organizations in Chapter 7, it was noted that "representative" consumer bodies can only be as good as their research staff. The research needed would not in many cases be very expensive. The gas and electricity Consultative Councils would certainly not need research staff in each Board Area. Some research could also be contracted out to universities, research organizations, and technical colleges, as Professor Robson has suggested.[10]

[8] *Report of the Committee of Enquiry into the Electricity Supply Industry* (the Herbert Committee) Cmd. 9672, 1956, paras. 446–447.

[9] *Consumer Protection and Enlightenment*, March 1960.

[10] *Nationalized Industry and Public Ownership*, pp. 264–265.

The variety of rather uninformative names under which the Councils operate constitutes a serious hindrance to wider public understanding of their functions. A legislative distinction was drawn between "consumers' councils" in the coal industry, and "consultative councils" in the gas and electricity industries and "consultative committees" in the transport industry on the grounds that in gas, electricity, and transport the councils should do more than represent consumers—"it was felt that it was as important for the Councils to interpret and explain the Boards' policies to consumers as it was for them to act as consumers' champions."[11] Whatever the basis of the distinction, a simple generic term such as "consumers' council" is undoubtedly needed to promote public understanding of their main purpose.

The electricity Consultative Councils have twenty to thirty members, of which at least two-fifths, and at most three-fifths, must be members of local authorities in the area. The gas Consultative Councils have the same number of members, of which one-third to three-quarters must be members of local authorities. In consequence, there are cases of Consultative Councils acting as pressure groups for the industries they represent, when these are of importance locally. The report of the Northern Gas Consultative Council for the year ending March 1961 states that "the Council was disappointed to learn that a local authority in the area, which had decided to adopt gas firing for heating installations in a teachers' training college, had received a request from the Ministry of Education that the system should be oil fired." The Minister later wrote that "while he remained of the opinion that an oil-fired installation was preferable because of the low running costs, he appreciated the desire to use a locally produced fuel and recognized that the extra annual cost was not high when viewed against the total cost of maintaining the college", and withdrew his request to use oil. The North of Scotland Hydro-Electricity Board Consultative Council in its report for the year ended December 1960 complained that "the merits of electricity, as compared with oil and other forms of fuel, for heating schools, hotels and hospitals were considered on several occasions and the Council was disappointed to note that preference is not always given to electricity as being the native product, where it is competitive with other fuels." Pressure of this sort may be a legitimate activity for producers' boards, but hardly for consumers' councils.

[11] The Herbert Committee (Cmd. 9672, 1956) para. 443.

4. *Consumer representation and price increases*

A complaints service can perform a useful function in almost any industry by maintaining two-way communication between producers and consumers. The more progressive private manufacturers and firms appreciate that a service of this kind can supplement market research and their sales figures in providing them with useful information about consumers' preferences. Generally speaking, the more efficient a firm and the more advanced the environment in which it is operating, the more genuine concern it will evince towards consumer satisfaction. While some American firms have undertaken investigations of post-purchase consumer dissatisfaction with their products, a field which is being studied under the title of "consumer dissonance",[12] very few firms outside the U.S.A. seem to have taken a sufficiently long-term view of their own interests to do so. So long as there is no producer-sponsored complaints organization, independent or statutory bodies of the type represented by the Consultative Committees in nationalized industries have a useful role to play. But it is misguided to give a complaints service a central or exclusive function in promoting the consumer's interest, and it is very doubtful whether complaints organizations should receive large public subsidies. The amount of public money which can be devoted to promoting consumers' interests is limited, and there are more pressing needs from the consumer's point of view than complaints machinery.

Consultative Councils would be much more useful if they could offer resistance to price increases. The Councils have not often opposed proposals for price increases, and where they have done so their protests, expectedly, have had little effect.

The response of the Coal Consumers' Councils to four major price increases by the National Coal Board from the early 1950's onward is fairly typical. "In April [1953] we felt it necessary to protest at the N.C.B.'s proposals for increasing prices from May 3rd in order to prevent the accumulated loss on their accounts from getting any bigger. . . . We deplored especially that while it appeared needful to increase coal prices generally the N.C.B. should propose to discriminate against householders by raising house coal more than industrial coal."

In 1955 the Domestic Coal Consumers' Council was apparently prepared to recommend a subsidy to keep down the price of coal.

[12] Bruce C. Straits, "The pursuit of the dissonant consumer", *Journal of Marketing*, July 1964, p. 62.

The Council had been advised by the N.C.B. that the Board intended to raise pithead prices by 8 per cent from June 1956, on top of the 18 per cent increase in 1955. The Council remarked: "Although we realized that the National Coal Board cannot continue indefinitely to operate at a loss, we must express our serious concern at the ever-increasing price of coal and the inflationary effect it must have on the general cost of living. This affects everybody and is a real hardship to old-age pensioners and others living on low incomes, many of whom depend upon an all-day fire for their bare comfort in winter."

In September 1960 another substantial price increase was proposed by the N.C.B. The Industrial Consumers' Council (addressing the Minister) said:

In the first place, we did not feel that, on the information at present available to us, we could really question the Board's view (and your own), that, faced with the costs of the various measures they decided to take and others over which they had no control, £60 million per annum was the least sum needed to balance their costs and provide a small margin for the Board to start reducing their accumulated deficit.

Neither could they come to any conclusion on a claim by the Iron and Steel Federation that the price increases discriminated against iron and steel in favour of the gas industry. The Domestic Coal Consumers' Council said on the same occasion:

The Board explained to us how their finances had been affected by various additions to their costs, and we regretfully accepted the need for increased revenue. We were of the opinion, however, that the rise in prices would lead to a further decline in sales of house coal.

In 1962 the Domestic Consumers' Council resolved that

this Council accepts with regret the need for an increase in the price of house coal, but recommends that the proposed larger increases in Scotland, Lancashire and North Wales should be abandoned in favour of a uniform price increase over the whole country, sufficient to bring in the same increase in revenue.

The gas and electricity Consultative Councils seem generally to have accepted their respective Boards' cases for price increases. Only two examples need be quoted. "The tariffs sub-committee were unanimous in their opinion that an increase in tariffs was necessary, although a minority of the members considered that the increase in the unit charge was too high." (Eastern Electricity Consultative Council, year ended March 1961.) "Having received very full explanations of your proposals and the reasons therefore from your Chairman, the Council approved your new tariff proposals, but with great reluctance." (Scottish Gas Consultative Council, year ended March 31st, 1961.)

In addition to the consumers' councils, supervision of the prices of the nationalized industries has been operated by the Ministries concerned on an informal basis. In the coal industry a "gentleman's agreement" between the coal owners and the government, entered into at the beginning of the Second World War and continued after nationalization, specified that the N.C.B. had to consult the Minister of Power before increasing prices, and until the late 1950's many of the N.C.B.'s requests for price increases were either deferred by the Minister or reduced in size, and in one case he rejected the application entirely.[13] A similar arrangement was operated in the gas and electricity industries, and the Select Committee on the Nationalized Industries has brought to light Ministerial influence on the fares of B.O.A.C. and B.E.A. However, in 1961 the White Paper on *The Financial and Economic Obligations of the Nationalized Industries* (Cmnd. 1337) established the principle that the nationalized industries must break even taking one year with another, and must also charge prices high enough to meet part of the cost of their investment programme (particularly in electricity, for they had not previously done so).

In general, the practice of Ministerial or other "political" supervision of the prices of the nationalized industries is deplorable. Apart from the fact that artificially low prices lead to a distortion of production, consumption, and investment in the economy as a whole, price increases are almost invariably only postponed, not abandoned. Thus the increase in coal and rail transport charges since the mid-1950's has been higher than it would have been if prices had not been kept down for political reasons in the preceding years.

5. Countervailing power in the nationalized sector

If political control of prices is ruled out what are the alternatives?

One way in which a consumer council in a nationalized industry

[13] W. A. Robson, *op. cit.*, p. 155.

could counter its Board's proposals for price increases would be by international comparisons of efficiency, by pointing out, for example, that an individual item in an industry's costs, or the industry's total costs, was significantly lower in another country. It seems likely, however, that a consumer council's research staff, even if suitably strengthened, would not be adequate for this very detailed and difficult type of research, which should be left to universities, research organizations, or the business organization itself.

What is needed is economic research of a simpler and more pragmatic kind. In the first place, the consumer council should keep continuous watch on *prices* of the product concerned in foreign countries. When a significant difference appeared in favour of foreign products, it would be empowered, and perhaps required, to press for an increase in imports. As far as the nationalized industries in Britain are concerned, the relevance of this line of action would be mainly to the fuel industries (it is technically possible to import electricity, and of course coal).

The council would also undertake detailed studies of the *cost to consumers* of different kinds of fuel. When a significant gain to consumers as a whole, or to a particular group of consumers, could be achieved by switching from one fuel to another, the council would see that the alternative was available and endeavour by publicity to persuade consumers to switch. The council should be required by its terms of reference to embark on this kind of publicity, whenever substantial gains would accrue to consumers from its doing so— *i.e.*, whenever a substantial price (or quality) difference emerged from its comparisons.

It is questionable whether, even if every likely improvement in staffing and organization were made, the present industry-based consumer councils could do much to offset price increases. A new approach is needed. One which comes immediately to mind is a proposal by Mr A. M. de Neumann in a study of the subject made before the existing councils had been in operation for very long.

Might not efficiency, success and economy of operation be better secured if there were, instead of the present functional structure of consumers' representation, a geographical structure with an independent council in each area, representing local consumers *vis-à-vis* all the nationalized industries? Such a grouping of councils, strongly reinforced by a really independent and well-endowed central research and information office of the highest standards, might be one of the solutions.[14]

Here may be the key to a solution, though for dealing with complaints of a routine nature the existing consultative councils might have to be retained, and the new body would probably have to be in addition to, not instead of, the existing ones. If we disregard the B.B.C., the Post Office, and the Bank of England, all in their own ways *sui generis*, as well as the steel industry, only part of which is nationalized, and which is subject to considerable competition from imports, the nationalized industries in Britain fall into two groups: fuel and energy (coal, gas, electricity, and atomic power) and transport (railways, and part of the civil aviation industry). Two consumer councils, each covering one of these groupings, would be able to provide the consumer with advice covering several competing services. Basically what is needed, however complicated may be the detailed working out, is advice to consumers on which services, for specified purposes, provide the best value for money.

The fuel industries would argue that this question is unanswerable, that it depends on the circumstances of the individual consumer, and that each fuel industry may, for certain uses, legitimately claim to give best value. However, even if it were true that in certain

[14] "Consumers' representation in the public sector of industry", *The Manchester School of Economic and Social Studies*, May 1950. A similar suggestion was made in 1952 by the (Ridley) Committee on National Fuel Policy (Cmd. 8647): "At the present time the public have to seek information on the merits of different fuels and fuel appliances from the suppliers of those fuels and appliances. Since the suppliers of the fuels are in competition, and appliance dealers often deal only in appliances for one type of fuel, the public will in practice rarely be able to obtain from one source a comprehensive and objective information service to help in the choice of fuel for a given purpose. . . ." "The Ministry of Fuel and Power should establish a source of information in each large town. . . . This service would be centred in the town hall and be provided with literature in which would be available data on a comparable basis on the capital and running costs and of the operating characteristics of the various fuels and appliances; these data would be compiled by the Ministry of Fuel and Power in consultation with the Building Research Station, Fuel Research Station and other official or semi-official bodies." (Paras. 260 and 261.)

The proposal for a centralized fuel research service has also been put forward by Mary Stewart, *Consumers' Councils*, Fabian Research Series No. 155, 1953; and by P. Sargent Florence and H. Maddick, "Consumers' Councils in the Nationalized Industries", *The Political Quarterly*, July–September 1953.

circumstances and for certain purposes different fuels may be best, it would be desirable that these circumstances should be defined and publicized. There would, indeed, be a strong case for a multi-industry advisory service of this kind in the fuel industries, and perhaps to a lesser extent in transport, even if the industries concerned were not nationalized.

An attempt to give the consumer the knowledge needed for a more effective choice might also be helped by an extension of the retailing activities of the nationalized industries, if the retail outlets disseminated information of an objective kind as well as their own sales promotion literature. An expansion of the (at present very small) retailing activities of the National Coal Board, and also of the Gas Boards, would be especially desirable in view of the unsatisfactory state of private merchandising of coal, coke, and smokeless fuels[15] (though the latter arises in part from the unwillingness of the manufacturers of these fuels—including the nationalized Boards—to give satisfactory information about their products). Such an extension would undoubtedly encounter strong opposition from established retail interests.

A multi-industry consumer research and advisory body of this kind would be able not only to "put the consumer's point of view" to the management of a nationalized industry but would be able to negotiate with it from a position of strength. It would be able to influence either favourably or adversely the sales of a particular fuel, and it should have the power to promote the use of competing products, such as oil and imported coal. The need for research and information on the merits of competing fuels is particularly great

[15] *cf.* reports on "Smokeless Solid Fuels", *Shopper's Guide* No. 26, May 1962; and *Which?* on "Coal Deliveries", December 1963, and "Coal", September 1964. The *Shopper's Guide* report stated that a moisture content of about 4 per cent is inevitable in the manufacture of most solid fuels, and some moisture is useful, but moisture contents of up to 30 per cent were found in the brands tested. Price was no guide to quality. The greatest heat value was as likely to be found in the lowest-priced fuels as in the highest.

Smokeless fuels, for which demand is growing as smoke control spreads, include anthracite, semi-bituminous coal, hard coke, gas coke, low-temperature cokes, and briquettes. They are manufactured by carbonizing coal, which is discharged from the oven in a red-hot state. It then has to be cooled, usually with water, and the water content of the fuel when sold can vary considerably. (In addition, it may later be stored in the open by the wholesaler or retailer.) The industrial buyer is aware of this and negotiates his terms with the seller accordingly, but the private consumer cannot do this and is offered no discount for the water content of his fuel purchase.

because once a consumer has installed a central-heating system it is extremely difficult to switch to a different type, and central heating is at present one of the most rapidly growing areas of consumer expenditure. Consumer information therefore needs to be linked with price *predictions* covering a period of, say, five years, to enable the consumer to decide which system would give the best value for money not only at present but at probable future prices. It might be feasible for consumer organizations to assist with publicity any fuel industry which could give a firm guarantee to cut prices, or not to raise them.

As in private industry publication of detailed profits figures can be a useful measure against monopoly, so in the nationalized sector published information can be a stimulus to efficiency. The railways could, for example, be obliged to publish statistics of the proportion of trains which exceed the times laid down in time-tables, and the times by which schedules are exceeded. Financial pressures by or on behalf of consumers could be considerably strengthened. In Japan, on certain long-distance trains, passengers have the right to claim a refund of a percentage of their fares if the trains are overdue.[16]

Returning to first principles, it is for consideration whether effort might not be better devoted to reducing the degree of monopoly of nationalized industries, and other "natural monopolies", rather than to methods of controlling or supervising their prices. And certainly nationalization with the object of creating a higher degree of monopoly than exists before nationalization (cement? insurance?) is greatly to be deplored. As mentioned, the monopoly position of the railways has been seriously undermined by the growth of road and air transport. Indeed, the railways can no longer be said to have a monopoly except in the special case of commuter transport to large cities, where it is desirable to discourage the private-car commuter and where public road transport could not carry the same volume of peak-hour passengers as the railways. The long-term remedy may be decentralization of employment, but in the meantime close public supervision of efficiency and prices of conurbation railway systems is essential.

In domestic air transport there has been a considerable reduction in the degree of monopoly of the nationalized air corporations since they were set up, and where foreign flights are concerned there is

[16] Letter in *The Times*, July 4th, 1968.

of course intensive competition, though the rules of the International Air Transport Association limit price competition and divert competition mainly into advertising. Probably the most important immediate scope for weakening a monopoly position lies in local bus services. Though these are not nationalized, the private or municipal companies which operate them usually have a monopoly within their own area. The accepted arguments for giving a local monopoly to bus operators are almost entirely without foundation.[17]

The long-term solution in the fuel and energy sector probably lies in technical developments such as fuel cells, discussed in the next chapter. These new developments would not only increase the degree of competition faced by the existing fuel industries but could eliminate one of the largest items in their costs, the "octopoid" distribution networks for electricity and gas. Pending such developments the electricity industry is likely to retain a high degree of monopoly for lighting and domestic energy purposes, though not for heating or cooking, and the case for public supervision is strong.

The electricity industry should not only be permitted, but *obliged*, to use the cheapest form of fuel in its generating-stations. It has a choice of gas, oil, coal, hydro-electricity, or nuclear power. At present there is little doubt that the first two are the preferred candidates. The purchasing power of the government and local authorities could also be used to prevent fuel and energy prices from rising, subject to the qualifications mentioned—the difficulty of switching from one heating system to another and the absolute monopoly which electricity has for some forms of energy consumption. The government might, for example, announce that for every 5 per cent rise in electricity prices an additional 10 per cent of heating installations in new government buildings would be diverted to a competing fuel, and the same principle might be extended to local authority housing. (If the price of another fuel showed a tendency to rise more than electricity prices, the sanctions would, of course, be reversed.)

[17] See the excellent discussion in John Hibbs, *Transport for Passengers*, Institute of Economic Affairs, Hobart Paper 23, 1963, pp. 25–36.

CHAPTER

9

Scientific and Industrial Research and the Consumer[1]

A technological revolution that bankrupts us all in the process is not much good to anyone. It is only too easy to lose money on innovation.

SIR DONALD STOKES,
Chief Executive of British Leyland Motor Corporation

1. *The need for a criterion*

Since early in the 1950's there has been concern in Britain, the U.S.A., and other countries over the question of whether adequate resources of money and manpower are being devoted to scientific research. Concern turned into something like panic after the launching of the first sputnik in 1957. During the same period there has been a sharp growth in spending on research, amounting almost to a research revolution. Between 1949–50 and 1959–60, according to estimates by the Federation of British Industries, research and development spending by manufacturing industry (at current prices) nearly quadrupled, to reach £250 million in the latter year. Between the same two years government spending on civilian industrial and scientific research rose from £5·2 million to £38·8 million, and rose further to £42·1 million in 1961–62.[2] Expenditure on research and

[1] "Research and development" is defined by the U.S. National Science Foundation as including "basic and applied research in the sciences (including medicine) and in engineering, and design and development of prototypes and processes. It does not include non-technological activities and technical service, such as quality control, routine product testing, market research, sales promotion, sales service, geological or geophysical exploration, or research in the social sciences of psychology." This definition is acceptable here, except that medical research is, in the main, outside the scope of the present discussion. In this chapter, "research" is frequently used to mean "research and development" (r. and d.).
[2] Federation of British Industries, "Industrial Research in Manufacturing Industry, 1959/1960", December 1961.

development of all kinds (civil and military, government and private) rose from about £300 million in 1955–56 to £700 million in 1963–4, and is expected to exceed £1000 million by 1970.[3]

Over the past two decades, growth in gross national product, in Britain or elsewhere, shows no obvious relation to the amount spent on research, and that some of the fastest growth rates have been achieved by countries which spend little on research. The main explanation is undoubtedly that research efforts have been heavily concentrated on aviation, atomic power, defence, and space exploration. "Prestige in foreign policy no longer rests on gunboats, but on the technical virtuosity of space satellites."[4]

Some passing references appear in government publications and in economic literature on the criteria for allocating research spending. The Advisory Council on Scientific Policy stated in its 1959–60 annual report:

> It is not possible to lay down a clear central direction as to how the national research effort should be distributed. It is clear that with our limited resources, both of manpower and finance, we cannot attempt to be active in every line of scientific activity . . . [The contribution of industry] must be along the lines which yield most remunerative returns. The government also has its part to play, particularly where responsibility is divided or unrecognized, and where the scope of the project is so large, that it falls outside the normal scope of industry. Both industry and government need to be very selective, and to avoid dissipating their resources by spreading them too thinly.

The 1960–61 report of the A.C.S.P. also touched on the question of priorities. *The Economist*[5] commented on that report: "The idea of arranging all these candidates for public importance pre-supposes a comprehensive science policy of a kind that no government has yet framed . . . The present arrangements encourage the suspicion that massive government aid goes to the best advocates and not necessarily to the best scientists." This pinpoints the question, but makes no attempt at an answer. Calls for a "national science policy" have since become more frequent.

By 1964 the A.C.S.P. like many other observers, seemed to have

[3] "Research and Development—Survey of the 60s", K. Grossfield and M. Zvegintzov, *National Provincial Bank Review*, August 1963.

[4] Mr K. Pavitt, of the Directorate for Scientific Affairs of the O.E.C.D., addressing the British Association for the Advancement of Science (Economics Section), September 1963.

[5] January 13th, 1962, p. 144.

arrived at one negative conclusion on allocation—*i.e.*, that the demands of atomic physics could not continue to be met on the present scale if as a result other areas of science were starved of manpower and resources—but seemed unwilling to say so directly. The last (1963–64) report of the Council,[6] before it was wound up, remarked:

> If our industry is to succeed [in selling goods abroad] it must get a fair share of men of the highest quality. Already much concern has been expressed about the tendency for too high a proportion of our best brains to go into pure research rather than into applied science and engineering . . . In the extreme, it would be just as foolish to develop pure research on such a scale that it absorbed all the high-grade manpower needed by industry as it would be to concentrate wholly on technology and eschew the acquisition of new scientific knowledge. And even within the field of pure science, due regard must be paid to the effect of magnifying unduly the effort in one area compared with others. It is for consideration, for example, how far a massive concentration on one area of pure physics would adversely affect our supply of first-class industrial physicists and engineers.

The academic literature is equally scanty and elliptical. Professors Carter and Williams[7] put forward two principles for government assistance to research: the policies of "reinforcing success", and of concentrating on weak points (the latter because technical backwardness tends to be self-perpetuating). The same authors justify government research in agriculture because the necessary research work is too large-scale to be done by farmers, and in atomic energy on three grounds: there was "a big problem with a solution in sight", "a strong prospect that the solution would be profitable", and "a virtual certainty that the task of seeking it was beyond the strength of private industry".

Two other principles have often been mentioned, and both are clearly relevant. One is that the State should intervene to fill the gaps in private research, where these can be detected. The other is that special attention should be given to industries which are actual or potential exporters (though we do not know which industries may become exporters in the future, and industries which *supply* export industries are equally important). Recently, the principle of

---

[6] December 1964, Cmnd. 2538, para. 24.

[7] *Science in Industry* (Oxford University Press, 1959, Chapter 9, "The Strategy of Government Aid").

import-saving has also been recognized. The criteria of promoting exports and "filling gaps" were stated in the 1952–53 report of the Advisory Council on Scientific Policy:

> In the absence of more detailed statistical information, it is almost impossible to express any detailed opinion about research in specific fields, or about the balance of the research effort between the various fields of work. The Royal Society in the field of pure scientific research, and the Research Councils[8] in their respective spheres, regard it as their function to insure that gaps in research are detected, and, if possible, filled.

The same report commented:

> Only 10 per cent. of U.K. exports (nylon, penicillin, new aircraft) are things which were unknown before the war. . . .Only continued emphasis on new and more efficient methods of production, and on new product development, can provide our manufacturing industry with the advantages it requires in the increasingly competitive world of international trade.

That increased scientific research in the past decade has had little effect on the standard of living is now fairly widely appreciated. At the popular level, there have been jokes about the co-existence of space travel and poor living conditions in Russia.[9] Confronted with this paradox, it is being realized that the direction of scientific research is as important as its total volume, even though there have been few constructive suggestions for re-allocation. One academic writer[10] has said:

> I think it is quite incontrovertible that there is no reason whatever to believe that the existing level of basic research by educational institutions, burdened by rapidly rising enrolments and rapidly rising research costs, by governments overwhelmingly interested in military advantage and by industry primarily concerned with short-term profits, bears any relation to the socially-desirable level.

[8] The Department of Scientific and Industrial Research, the Agricultural Research Council, the Medical Research Council, the Nature Conservancy.
[9] A caller at a house asks the child: "Where is your father?" "He is circling the earth in a space ship and will not be back till the evening." "Where is your mother?" "She is shopping for meat and will not be back till the evening."
[10] H. H. Villard, "Competition, Oligopoly and Research", *Journal of Political Economy*, December 1958.

At the very least, it seems to be indisputable that the level of basic research needs to be determined more by conscious policy and that the whole matter deserves far more careful attention than it currently receives.

It is, indeed, not impossible that large centrally-directed research programmes have been harmful to the consumer, the standard of living, and the rate of economic growth, by absorbing resources of capital and scientific manpower which would otherwise have been available over a much wider field. Almost inevitably government research programmes are motivated by considerations of prestige rather than of profit; hence the Concorde airliner, while the most profitable branches of the aircraft industry have been

standardized jets carefully tailored to the commercial market; the engine-makers, like Rolls Royce, have been able to make profits from being able to fit the new engines to a wider range of new and re-conditioned frames; while smaller companies, including now Handley Page, have been able to tap the huge world potential for reliable aircraft at a modest price. At the bottom end there is probably no activity in the industry so generally profitable as the intelligently conducted supply of spares.[11]

It is also an established feature of government research projects that when costs escalate, it is difficult to cut short the project without a political scandal, and there is strong pressure to throw good money after bad. Such problems may be less pressing in the U.S.A. Even in prestige projects, *eventually* useful results may materialize. The wrong approach can be highly damaging in countries where national, and research, resources are much more limited.

However, for present purposes we assume that, for good or ill, governments will continue to have at their disposal large sums for investment in research, and that the problem is how to make the best use of them.

2. *Consumer-orientated research*
The consumer interest in allocating research expenditure could be interpreted in various ways. Studies might be made of deficiencies in the supply of goods and services which for one reason or another have not been remedied by producers. Market research should have a considerable part to play in deciding how scientific research could

[11] George Cyriax, "Getting profits into new ideas", *The Financial Times*, September 22nd, 1966.

K

promote consumer satisfaction, though to do so it would have to be to a greater extent than at present in the hands of universities and independent social and economic research organizations. Even then its possibilities are more limited than might appear at first sight. This is so partly because of the fact that consumers are inevitably limited in their knowledge and experience. Consumers obviously cannot say what goods not at present invented or marketed they would like to buy.[12] But even with goods actually available, their experience may be too limited to make constructive proposals. Thus, market research in the conventional sense, even if carried out by a wholly disinterested body, would have to be supplemented by "functional" research into consumers' behaviour—that is to say, the use or purpose of the commodity concerned would have to be taken as the starting-point of investigation. For example: a consumer's expressed wish for a vacuum cleaner might be better met by an effortless means of getting rid of dust, or a type of floor covering which repelled dust; for heating might be met by better heat insulation in buildings; for a car might be met by better public transport, or forms of transport not yet in use—e.g., moving pavements.

Market research could certainly find out what consumers consider to be defective in the existing supply of goods and services and provide an indication for the direction of research. So could information on consumers' complaints. Detailed analysis of figures of accidents in the home could provide guidance for research designed to improve safety.

Another approach to the problem of directing scientific and industrial research into the channels most useful to consumers would be to use it to stimulate new products in competition with monopolies. The importance of innovation in reducing monopoly power has been stressed in Chapter 4. Similarly, scientific research could be directed to finding low-priced substitutes, the need for which was discussed in Chapter 6.

Yet another approach would be to aim at allocating research spending in rough accordance with the categories of consumer expenditure, or to use scientific research deliberately to reduce prices

[12] A Christmas competition among *Observer* readers on what new inventions they would like to see (the results were published in the paper on January 19th, 1964) produced what the organizers of the competition admitted to be disappointingly few new ideas. The first prize went to a reader who suggested automated haircutting.

or prevent price increases. These two criteria are further examined in this chapter.

Some problems must be noted in advance.

(*a*) The criteria can be applied only to a very limited extent to the capital goods industries, since research in a capital goods industry benefits a wide range of consumer goods industries.[13] Research is in fact very heavily concentrated in the capital goods industries in Britain and the U.S.A., but this fact is probably mainly to be explained by the concentration of research spending on defence and prestige industries.

(*b*) It could well be argued that scientific research is a consumer good to which an advanced society has a right, perhaps an obligation, to devote a certain proportion of its collective spending.

(*c*) The efficiency of research spending, like that of other factors of production, can be increased—*e.g.*, by the use of computers. Scientists' productivity can be considerably increased by efficient information collection, storage, and retrieval systems. Further, there are likely to be economies of scale in many branches of scientific research.

(*d*) At least as important as spending is the type of research carried on, and implicit in the argument being developed here is the view that the research should be mainly of a kind which reduces costs and prices. An essential preliminary, therefore, would be a scientific-economic study of existing and potential research projects to discover which would be most likely to prove successful in achieving cheaper methods of production.

With all these qualifications in mind, we confront expenditure on

[13] "Excluding aircraft, at least four-fifths of both research expenditure and scientific manpower is spread over only six industries which support less than half the total employment in manufacturing industry: chemicals, electrical engineering, man-made fibres, general engineering (including instruments), metal manufacture and vehicles."—F.B.I. Report, "Industrial Research in Manufacturing Industry, 1959/60", p. 7). "The industrial pattern of research expenditure is strikingly similar in Britain and America. In both countries one group of industries—mainly capital goods and chemicals— account for over nine-tenths of research expenditure, though they employ a good deal less than half manufacturing industry's labour force." N.I.E.S.R., *Economic Review*, May 1962, "Research and development: a comparison between British and American Industry." In the same article it is claimed that "Research will tend to be concentrated in producer goods industries since it is essentially through the improvement of producer goods—machines and materials—that progress is achieved."

scientific and industrial research with, firstly, consumers' expenditure, and secondly, the trend of consumer prices.

Research spending, and household expenditure on the main categories of consumer buying, as given in the Ministry of Labour's
"Family Expenditure Survey", are compared in Table 1. The
Ministry's categories "alcoholic drink", "tobacco", "durable household goods", "services", and "miscellaneous expenditure" are not
included, "durable household goods" because it is not possible to
split the research expenditure of the engineering industries into
"capital" and "consumer" goods, and the other four categories for
obvious reasons. Research in the aircraft and ship-building industries
has not been included in "transport".

TABLE 1

	Consumer Spending (1959/61, three year average)			Research Spending (1959/60)	
	s.	d.	%	£ thousand	%
Housing	30	8·3	14	3,300	8
Fuel, Light, and Power	19	9·4	8	7,476	19
Food	101	9·4	47	13,272	27
Clothing and Footwear	33	2·6	15	8,302	20
Transport and Vehicles	33	11·5	16	10,959	26
	219	5·2	100	43,309	100

The comparison would indicate a substantial increase in house
(i.e., building) research and in research spending in food, at the
expense of research in fuel, light, and power, and in transport and
vehicles.

The second approach, confronting research spending with increases in consumer prices (over the period January 1956 to
January 1962) would indicate increases in research spending on
housing and fuel, light and power at the expense of the other
categories. Between the two dates the index of retail prices rose by
17½ points. The housing component of the index rose by 40 per cent,
and the fuel and light component by 30 per cent, compared with
27 per cent in transport and vehicles, 12½ per cent in food, 6½ per
cent in clothing and footwear, and 2 per cent in household durable
goods.[14]

[14] Central Statistical Office, *Economic Trends*, July 1962.

3. *Building Research*

Concurrently with the rise in house prices which has taken place since the mid-1950's, there has been intensified interest in building with the prospect of further increases in the near future. Compared with its previous condition, the building industry is now in a veritable ferment of research activity and new ideas.

From 1960 onward, a number of official studies were made into the construction industry, as it became clear that the industry was not likely to increase its output as rapidly as the projected demand for housing, civil engineering and road building, and commercial building. The Ministry of Works' "Survey of problems before the construction industries" (the Emmerson Report) 1962, noted that nearly half the total capital investment of the country in building was on public account, and "the Government needs to exercise a more positive influence on the general efficiency of the industry." It also recommended greater standardization of materials and components; more co-ordination between the building owners and the professions; expanded training facilities; more research and information; and more consultation between the government and the construction industry.

In 1964 a Working Party on Building Research and Information Services recommended a levy on the construction industry for research and information services. The annual sum to be raised from the industry should be £500,000 in the first year. The total annual budget, according to the Working Party, should build up to £3 million within five years, and about £5 million in the longer run, in addition to existing research and development expenditure. In deciding that building research and development was inadequate, the Working Party used the simple criterion of r. and d. as a percentage of total sales by the industry. For industry as a whole, r. and d. as a percentage of sales value was 2·7 per cent in 1960–61 while in construction and its supplying industries it was only 0·3 per cent, £10 million divided by £3,000 million. The figure of £10 million existing research spending was arrived at by adding:

£3 million for research, development, and advisory services in the construction industry; £2 million for research in the glass, cement, and ceramics industries; £5 million for research in the metals, plastics, and paints, and other materials industries.

Comparing research expenditure to total output is, if anything, even more arbitrary than the procedures adopted in the preceding section; but, by this criterion also, a substantial rise in r. and d. spending in the building industry is indicated.

If we perhaps over-generously include the estimate of the research spending by the *supplying industries* of the construction industry, the £10 million above has still to be divided by about three to arrive at the sum which can be allocated to building research in the *housing* sector of the construction industry (about one-third). Thus we get a figure of £3·3 million for existing spending, which the government proposed to increase by £1·7 million (one-third of the £5 million for the whole construction industry).

4. *"Fall-out" from Military Research*

In favour of military and prestige programmes of scientific research, it is frequently, and correctly, stated that they bring benefits in the form of civilian "fall-out". A comprehensive examination of the civilian side-effects of military research cannot be attempted here but some recent examples may be listed.

From military research before and during the Second World War sprang synthetic rubber, new adhesives, and sea-sickness remedies, on which intensive study was undertaken before D-Day. Research on clothing and boots, especially in connection with durability, has helped civilian production. The confectionery industry benefited from the results of German research into the "keeping" qualities of chocolate. Many workshop techniques developed for the production of weapons have been adopted for engineering use. Containers developed during the war in connection with parachute drops of military stores have been adopted for safe transit of fragile materials and equipment. From wartime research came radar, with its contribution to sea and air travel, and minor uses such as locating shoals of fish. The most important single by-product was, of course, atomic power.

The aircraft industry has benefited greatly from the military aviation programme, in which the stress has been on greater speed, greater load-carrying capacity, and longer range. Work in many related fields, such as light-weight metals, has thereby been stimulated. In communications the most spectacular results of military scientific research—space satellites and Telstar—have evolved. Among developments which should, for the consumer's sake, be given the utmost encouragement are those which will make possible decentralizing of work as communications improve, so eliminating the housing-transport cost squeeze on the commuter.[15]

Important medical advances are claimed to have resulted from the space race. Light-weight sensors developed to measure heart activity: breathing, brain waves, and other bodily functions of astronauts have been adopted for hospital use, so that patients can be monitored electronically. Better hearing aids, radar for the blind, and artificial limbs can be made using electronic circuits. A number of more specialized medical developments are in prospect, such as pressurized space suits for patients with blood-pressure problems.

But in other cases it is practically impossible to say whether or not a particular development was or was not the result of pressure of military needs. Improved weather forecasting, which has had beneficial economic effects in farming, fishing, and sea and air transport has been partly due to military needs but probably most of this would have come independently. One author holds that several of the developments in civilian science claimed to have originated from space research have not in fact done so, and the process has been in the reverse direction.[16]

Many scientific discoveries, including plastics, synthetic fibres, synthetic detergents, fertilizers, and most pharmaceuticals, owe little or nothing to military research. The computer and the transistor

[15] One attempt to peer into the near distance states: "As communications improve, so the need for transportation will decrease. Our grandchildren will scarcely believe that millions once spent hours of every day fighting their way into city offices—where, as often as not, they did nothing that could not have been achieved over telecommunication links . . . The business of the future may be run by executives who are scarcely ever in each other's physical presence. It will not even have an address or a central office—only the equivalent of a telephone number. For its files and its records will be space rented in the memory units of computers that could be stored anywhere on Earth; the information stored on them could be read off on high-speed printers whenever any of the firm's officers needed it." Arthur C. Clark, *Profiles of the Future* (Pan Books, London, 1962).

[16] "The telemetry system that reports on the physical responses of astronauts in flight has been adopted for a remote-control system monitoring patients in a Detroit hospital, proclaim N.A.S.A. press agents. 'I'm afraid it's the other way round,' remarks Dr. F. A. Albert, the Hospital's director of psychophysiology. 'We have been working in the field since 1948 and our application has been found to be useful in the space programme.'" Amitai Etzioni, *The Moon-doggle: Domestic and International Implications of the Space Race* (Doubleday & Co., New York, 1964), p. 78.

owed little to military research in their formative stages. The Mark 1 digital computer produced at Harvard in 1944 combined for the first time a number of earlier inventions—data processing machines, magnetic recording on steel tape, and flexible plastics. Further development of the computer depended on transistors, as the early computers were bulky, expensive, unreliable, and difficult to maintain. The transistor itself was largely the result of advances in basic (solid-state) theory, and in fundamental research by the American Telephone and Telegraph Company, in whose Bell Laboratories it was first produced in 1948. Perhaps, in the long run, the most important outcome of scientific research for military use has been a more widespread interest in research as such, and an appreciation that there are few practical problems which cannot be solved if they are tackled scientifically.

In the U.S.A., intensive efforts have been made to maximize civilian fall-out from defence research, especially that undertaken by the National Aeronautics and Space Administration. It has been stipulated that all patents arising out of work for the N.A.S.A. shall be government property and open to all, and seven independent research centres have been commissioned to process and appraise for civilian use the innovations—about 1500 a year—which emerge from N.A.S.A. But the results to date are reported to be small, and the applications mainly in the future.

As military and space technology advance, the gap between them and civilian technology increases to such an extent that the derivative fall-out becomes progressively smaller relative to the resource input. According to Dr Jerome Wiesner, President Kennedy's science adviser, "There is not nearly as direct an application of the Atlas Booster (rocket) to the civilian economy as there was of the B.52 (bomber) to the (Boeing) 707 . . . In the future there will not be nearly the same direct impact of military and space research on the civilian economy."[17]

It is, after all, not surprising that an investment programme, however large, directed to one particular end has not made more progress towards quite different ends. It has been traditional to express doubt as to whether scientific research would or could be directed at all; it is one of the clichés of scientific history that many discoveries have come as by-products of work directed to other objectives. "Basic advances in science cannot be predicted, and the theory that such progress can be produced simply by pouring in money and resources

[17] Etzioni, *The Moon-doggle*, pp. 84–85.

is without foundation."[18] But in applied research and in development, the correlation may be rather closer. The advances in military and space technology which have come about in recent years are certainly a direct consequence of the scale of the research effort devoted to them. By the law of averages, a sufficiently large input of research spending is likely to bring results in almost any field, though the success of any individual project remains a gamble.

An example of research which would not duplicate research being done in the U.S.A. is the magnetohydrodynamic method of generating electricity, as an alternative to nuclear power. MHD would replace the rotating electrical conductors of a conventional generator with a jet of hot, fast-moving gas. The chairman of the Central Electricity Generating Board has commented: "One of the things which is worrying me at the moment about MHD is that, in the absence of a nuclear programme, I would say without hesitation that we should go vigorously ahead with research on MHD; this is going to give you higher efficiency, though at higher capital costs. Without a nuclear programme, while there would be a lot of problems in MHD, I am sure they could be solved with sufficient research, and I am certain it would be right to go ahead and solve them."[19] Tidal and solar energy, fuel cells, storage batteries, and home thermal generators are other obvious alternatives to nuclear power for civilian use. While no one country could follow up all these lines, there is a case for international division of labour whereby each country selected and followed one of them, as an alternative to research on nuclear energy.

5. Conclusion

An examination of the allocation of civilian research spending in Britain between industry groups suggests that building research, and perhaps power and food research, should be increased at the expense of other groups. Building research should be nearly doubled from its 1959–60 level of some £3·3 million if consumer expenditure is taken as the criterion, and should be increased even more if we adopt the criterion of using research to counter price increases. If the latter were adopted building research should receive the largest share of the £43 million spent in 1959–60 on the commodity groups examined. Other individuals and organizations have also come to the not very

[18] Advisory Council on Scientific Policy, 1959/60 Annual Report.
[19] New Scientist, July 23rd, 1964. The C.E.G.B. has in fact initiated a £2 million research programme in MHD.

recondite conclusion that building research ought to be increased, and, as noted in section 3 of this chapter, there has indeed been some increase in building research in the intervening years, with the prospect of a further increase.

We may now drop our limiting assumption that the amount of money available for civilian research is fixed and look at the whole question in perspective. Total research spending is rising rapidly, having more than doubled between 1955 and 1964, from some £300 million to some £700 million, and is expected to surpass £1000 million (at 1964 prices) by 1970. In these circumstances, increased building research should not be regarded as research diverted from other consumer goods. It may be unrealistic to say that building research should be increased to £240 million a year, the sum spent by the U.K. Government on aircraft research, or £100 million a year, the sum spent at one time on atomic energy; but not to say that it should be increased to £40 or £50 million, over ten times its present volume, the State making up the difference between this sum and the research spending of private industry. Neither would it be unrealistic to argue that the same amount should be spent on one line of energy research other than nuclear power (tidal or solar energy, thermal storage or fuel cells) where a breakthrough is likely.

The coincidence of the needs of the domestic consumer and the national balance-of-payments criterion is again clear. If the large increase in research spending in Britain over the past fifteen years has contributed little to economic growth, still less has it contributed to exports. Percipient observers have noted that the most successful exporting countries, Germany, Italy, and Japan, spend relatively little on research, and that the largest spenders—Britain, France, and the U.S.A.—are consistently or intermittently poor performers in the export field. The prime reason is obvious. More than 70 per cent of the funds spent by the governments of the latter three countries is spent on defence, nuclear energy, and space research. If, however, building research were greatly increased, and if as a result cheap fittings, components, and perhaps whole buildings could be manufactured, and even more if use of plastics, aluminium, and other light-weight materials reduced transport costs, a revolutionized building industry could make a vast contribution to exports. Potential demand is evident in that no country in the world has solved its housing problem, and that the process of urbanization in under-developed countries is still in its early stages.

The export potential of cheap power from storage batteries or fuel cells, eliminating the costly physical distributive network of conventional or nuclear electricity and providing a cheap and portable means of heating, lighting, and cooking, is evident. In general, any product of considerable benefit to the consumer in Britain would find an equally ready export market in other advanced countries. For exporting to under-developed countries (and as a useful form of aid) research spending could be directed into channels specifically designed to answer their needs. With a little imagination a list of projects could rapidly be produced. Desalination of sea water is an obvious candidate. So is the whole area of irrigation techniques.

The requisite combination of knowledge of consumers' needs, export demand, and scientific and technical possibilities is beyond any one individual, and what seems to be called for in the first instance is a team of economists (including market researchers) and scientific and technical experts to draw up a list of projects.[20]

NOTE TO CHAPTER 9

Sources and method of construction of Table 1
(a) *Family expenditure* from figures in Ministry of Labour's "Family Expenditure Survey: report for 1962", Table 1 (all households).
(b) *Research expenditure*; figures for private firms' and research associations' spending are from Table 13, p. 102 of Federation of British Industries' "Industrial Research in Manufacturing Industry, 1959/60" (published December 1961). This inquiry is the only source of detailed information on non-governmental research spending in Britain. The figures for government spending are from Appendix D of the annual report of the Advisory Council on Scientific Policy, 1960/61, figures for year ending March 30th, 1960.

[20] Little attention has been devoted in this chapter to the suggestions which are usually made on probable innovations in personal and domestic consumption goods—home newspapers; robots for doing routine household tasks such as scrubbing, cleaning, shoe-polishing, and making beds; personal television-sets; personal "walkie-talkie" radio-sets; disposable clothing and crockery; heated clothing. Most of these will no doubt come eventually, with beneficial effects, but they are a field for private research spending on the usual commercial criteria.

The totals are made up as follows (£000):

	Private firms	Research Associations	Government	Total
Housing				3,300 (a)
Fuel, light, and power			773 (b)	8,249 (c)
Food	2,455 (d)	238 (d)	8,991 (e)	11,684
Clothing and footwear	6,846 (f)	1,496 (f)	—	8,342
Transport and vehicles	10,607 (g)	192 (g)	464 (h)	11,263

(a) From Report on Building Research and Information Services.

(b) Ministry of Power.

(c) Research expenditure of Gas Council (£847,000), National Coal Board (£2,427,000), Electricity Council (£2,202,000), and Central Electricity Generating Board (£2,000,000): total £7,476,000; plus item (b).

(d) Food manufacturing industries (food, baking, fruit and vegetable canning).

(e) Section A, "Agriculture, Forestry, Fisheries and Food", of Appendix D to Report of Advisory Council on Scientific Policy, with figures for forestry extracted.

(f) Textiles, leather, and footwear.

(g) Motor industry only.

(h) Road Research Laboratory and Ministry of Transport.

10

Obsolescence in Consumer Goods

> The fashion wears out more apparel than the man.
> *Much Ado About Nothing*, Act III, Sc. 3.

1. *"Planned obsolescence"?*

Apart from housing, furniture, cooking utensils, the first modern consumer durable goods,[1] the sewing machine, the bicycle, and the typewriter, appeared towards the end of the nineteenth century. None of these have suffered from any high degree of model obsolescence, nor have there been complaints that manufacturers artificially shorten their life to maintain replacement sales; nor have there been any widespread and serious problems concerning repairs. There are, no doubt, explanations of these facts other than the deliberate design of manufacturers. They were introduced at a time when the income of the mass of consumers was not sufficiently high to ensure a strong replacement demand, and they are not in themselves technically complicated enough to make repairs a serious problem. The radio, motor-car, refrigerator, washing machine,

---

[1] There is a problem in defining "durable goods." Clothing is certainly durable, and even food is not usually consumed at the time of purchase. However, the ordinary distinction between durable and non-durable consumer goods is adequate for most practical purposes, although furniture is often not included in durable goods. "Durability" as a desirable attribute (the sense here used) in its simplest sense refers mainly to mechanical items (domestic equipment, cars, lawn-mowers, etc.). In shoes, clothing, carpets, furniture, upholstery, etc. at least as important as physical durability is retention of appearance. Thus, a carpet may not wear through to the backing (the usual criterion of durability) for a long time but may lose its appearance much more rapidly. Shrink resistance and fade resistance are of major importance in textiles. Ideally, a criterion or measure of durability must, for these items, include retention of appearance.

television-set, record-player, and home-movie set have been less fortunate.

It is sometimes alleged that useful inventions are suppressed in order to maintain the profitability of products already on the market. "Some years ago", wrote George Orwell in 1937,[2] "someone invented a gramophone record which would last for decades. One of the big gramophone-record companies bought up the patent rights, and that was the last that was ever heard of it." Another example frequently cited in support of such claims was the everlasting match, the patents of which were alleged to have been suppressed by the large match companies. The Monopolies Commission's report on the match industry[3] showed that an agreement on re-ignitable patents had been made in 1935, but that by 1952 the small numbers of re-ignitable patents held by Swedish Match were believed by the latter to be "of very little value" and the agreement had lapsed. There has, however, been no spectacular development since then in the production of "everlasting matches". (Flint gas lighters, not to mention cigarette-lighters, have of course been available all the time, but show no sign of superseding matches, presumably because of the weight of the former and the expense of the latter.)

None of these cases has been proved, and the National Research Development Corporation, which was set up in 1948 to exploit inventions which had not found a commercial developer, has discovered no likely inventions neglected, still less suppressed. All its work so far has consisted in developing its own inventions.

Many people believe that manufacturers design a durable good so as to break down at the end of a short period in order to maintain replacement sales. Implicit in this is the assumption that the physical life of such products could be lengthened without affecting the price. The strength with which this view is held in many quarters is undoubted evidence of widespread dissatisfaction with the performance of consumer durables, and the need for more attention to physical life on the part of manufacturers, as well as to better quality control. However, it seems on the face of it improbable that a manufacturer would adopt such a policy unless he had a complete monopoly of the market for the product. If he had not, the chances

---

[2] *The Road to Wigan Pier*, Penguin edn. (1962), p. 181.
[3] *Report on the Supply and Export of Matches and the Supply of Match-Making Machinery*, H.M.S.O., May 1953 (pp. 46–51).

are that the replacement sale would go to a competitor. A variation of the argument, put forward by some design experts, is that manufacturers do (or should) design a piece of equipment so that all the components break down simultaneously. Such a policy might be rational not only from the manufacturer's point of view but from the consumer's. If this policy existed it would be highly desirable that consumers should be notified of the expected life of the product, but there is very little evidence that it does.

Conceivably, manufacturers might make an explicit or implicit agreement to keep the physical life of all brands of a product short, but no evidence of such an agreement has come to light. Finally, there are innovations which have notably increased durability in certain consumer goods. Such as reinforced nylon men's socks (of one brand of which Leslie Adrian in the *Spectator* remarked, "they are so good that it is surprising that any other brands are on the market"[4]) and stainless-steel razor blades, of which the first was Wilkinson Sword. Transistors considerably improved durability and ease of maintenance in all areas in which they have been applied, the main one to date in the consumer-goods field being radios. Substituting synthetic fibres for wool in clothing, furnishing fabrics, carpets, etc., has resulted in a gain in durability in some respects, especially reduction of the danger from moths.

To dispute the "profits from rapid replacement" argument is not to imply that producers cannot profit from sub-standard durable goods. This is so because of consumer ignorance (the consumer may be unaware of the life of alternative brands, and may buy the product too infrequently to learn from experience) and a producer in a large market may rely entirely on new rather than replacement sales. It has been remarked that there are 200 million opportunities for selling a defective product in the U.S.A.—though even this may be small for a manufacturer aiming at long-term profits. In any case, it is still true that even with such a large market a producer cannot benefit from *replacement* sales through short product life. The opportunities for deception lie with people buying the product for the first time.

It might be true that the physical life of durable goods is unnecessarily short (*i.e.*, could be increased without raising the price) irrespective of the manufacturer's intentions, and the absence of any deliberate policy such as is assumed in the more naïve theories of

4 April 20th, 1962.

planned obsolescence. The main remedy here must lie in comparative testing[5] and the wider dissemination of test results, plus labelling by durability whenever practicable. Durability can be tested either by laboratory tests or by actual wear. One of the main problems is that different laboratory tests may give slightly different results and that tests may give somewhat different results from those of actual wear, a problem encountered in producing a durability standard for carpets. However, there is no reason to suppose that such standards are impracticable or that slight differences in results need cause serious problems in differentiating products into, say, three standard grades of durability.

2. *Fashion changes*

If we reject the "conspiracy" thesis that the physical life of products is deliberately kept short, there are still adequate grounds for concern about the life-span of consumer durables. These include fashion changes and after-sales service.

If manufacturers do not aim from the outset at keeping the life of a product short, they can produce the same effect by inspired fashion changes. There are many examples of fashion changes which are quite unexpected and independent of producers. Such was the case with leather boots as an article of women's fashion, which took the leather and shoe industries by surprise in 1962. There are also many examples of unsuccessful attempts by producers to initiate fashion changes. Nevertheless fashion changes are well established in many industries as a means of raising sales, and the number of industries in which this is true is increasing. Evidence is easily available in trade magazines and has been collated by a number of authors, notably by Vance Packard in *The Waste Makers*. In a great number of industries, manufacturers have been inspired by the examples of the clothing and automobile industries to introduce an element of regular fashion change in order to stimulate sales; cases in point include men's clothing, furniture, and kitchen equipment (where in the U.S.A. blue-coloured appliances were used in an attempt to make white appliances obsolete).

Many people don't know when their bed is worn out and too many think the 'rut' they are sleeping in is luxury, delegates at the National Bedding Federation's conference at Eastbourne were told

---

[5] Consumer testing organizations have, of course, done a considerable amount of work involving durability.

yesterday. The trouble is that a fine bed is not a status symbol, Mr Ivor Dennes, bedding buyer for Plummer Roddis Ltd, Brighton, told the conference. It is something which is not seen by visitors. It can be covered up and kept out of sight in the bedroom. Mr Dennes was one of a panel representing bedding manufacturers, retailers and customers who discussed the question: "Are Britons mean about their beds?" at the closing session of the conference at the Grand Hotel.[6]

Indeed, it is so obviously in the manufacturers' and retailers' interest to introduce fashion changes where none previously existed that detailed documentation would be tedious and supererogatory.

Is it in the general interest? It could be argued that producers are entitled to use any legal method of increasing sales open to them, and that fashion changes are no different in kind from any other sales promotion methods, including advertising. In the attempt to accelerate fashion changes, consumers may appear to be accomplices, if occasionally unwilling ones. Nevertheless the attempt to universalize fashion change in the consumer goods field substantially diminishes consumer choice, unnecessarily raises prices, and induces consumers to misallocate their spending. There is also strong evidence that where goods need maintenance and after-sales service it substantially reduces the efficiency of these services. It should, therefore, be discouraged.

Astonishingly, only one serious attempt seems to have been made to ascertain the cost of model changes. The results are given in an article in the *American Economic Review*, June 1962, by Messrs Fisher, Griliches, and Kaysen, "The Cost of Automobile Model Changes in the U.S.A. since 1949". They attempted to determine the cost of resources that would have been saved had cars of the 1949 model, length, weight, horsepower, and transmission been produced in every succeeding year up to 1960. They note that "as there was technological change in the industry, we are thus assessing not the resource expenditure that would have been saved had the 1949 models themselves been continued, but rather the resources that would have been saved had cars with 1949 specifications been continued but been built with the developing technology as estimated after actual car-construction costs and performance data." They conclude that the cost of model changes, excluding technological improvements, added $560 million a year to the industry's costs,

6 *Evening Argus* (Brighton), April 24th, 1964.

L

amounting to more than 25 per cent of the purchase price. This figure relates purely to construction costs, and does not allow for higher maintenance costs, especially the higher fuel consumption of the larger cars; and one aspect that the authors do not mention is that, as previously noted, rapid model changes undoubtedly add to the difficulties retailers and consumers experience as regards repairs and spare parts.

The conclusion is:

In thus assessing the costs of automobile model changes, we do not mean to deny that such changes also brought benefits. Indeed, it is quite clear that most or all of the changes involved were desired by the consuming public (perhaps after advertising) and that the automobile companies were satisfying such desires. Nevertheless the costs estimated seem so staggeringly high that it seems worth while presenting the bill and asking whether it was "worth it", in retrospect.

3. *The case for limited durability*
More rapid obsolescence might in certain circumstances be economically rational. The first complicating factor is income elasticities of demand (the percentage increase in expenditure on a given commodity when consumers', or national, income rises by a given percentage amount). It is a well-known fact that for the major consumer durables this is higher than unity—*i.e.*, for each ten per cent rise in their incomes consumers will increase by more than ten per cent their spending on the classic durables, cars, television-sets, washing machines, refrigerators, etc. But this provides little if any justification for induced fashion changes. These changes are taken by economists as given, as a basis for predicting economic trends, and it is no part of the predictive economists' job to say that trends should not be different from what they are. In any case, the high demand for durable goods may prove to be characteristics of only a limited stage of economic growth, and in the long term consumers may turn out to be even more avid for foreign holidays, better health and education, and more leisure and leisure activities.

Among new products likely to come into use in the future are crockery for use once and then thrown away, thereby saving effort on washing up (though infra-red rays for effortless washing up may provide an alternative solution) and clothing made from paper and thrown away after a short use period, thereby saving cleaning and repair expenditure. Paper kitchen towels and paper handkerchiefs have already to some extent displaced the traditional products. However, if such products are technically and economically feasible (*e.g.*, if cheap paper clothing can be produced which feels and looks the same as traditional clothing) they should be regarded as genuine innovations, rather than as acceleration of the degree of obsolescence of the old product. With a higher rate of technical and scientific progress, a higher rate of innovation of consumer goods is to be expected. It could be argued that model changes give manufacturers the opportunity of introducing more frequent improvements. Here the above argument would apply—there is no intention of stopping genuine innovation, but only of separating the genuine from the spurious. Indeed, a reduction in regular fashion changes would make it easier for consumers to see when a genuine product improvement has been made and to react accordingly. The few genuine changes in car design tend to be overlooked in the publicity surrounding the annual model change.

If repair charges rise more rapid replacement may become the rational alternative economically. The increasing cost of labour may in fact have this effect on repair charges in many products. It could also be argued that the inefficiency of repair services for most commodities makes it a more rational proceeding to buy a new commodity rather than expend the money, energy, and time that is needed to get something repaired. The probable higher cost of repairs is a valid reason for predicting a shorter durability for many products. The second point is also valid at present, but clearly the desirable solution is more efficient repair services.

Lastly, it can be argued that in housing, and perhaps in some other industries, more, not less obsolescence is needed if manufacturers are to take advantage of the economies of large-scale production. If housing is to become a mass-production industry in the same way as motor-cars and domestic electrical appliances, with cost and price savings similar to what has been achieved in these, it might be necessary, concomitantly with the introduction of industrialized building methods, for the average life of a house to be reduced and output increased to two or three times the present rate of 400,000 houses a year in the United Kingdom. There is a limited amount of experience—mainly that of West Germany—tending to show that increased output in housing will similarly bring economies of large-scale production. In theory the same object could be achieved by greater concentration of production in the industry, or perhaps by enforced standardization—legal requirements as to the dimensions of components and structural parts. However, development of mass production in an industry has invariably been increased by a rapid increase in total output, not mainly by concentration among existing firms; and also it may be that the mass-production firms are usually newcomers, so that a net increase in output is needed.

All this may be true, and yet may be largely irrelevant to the solution of the housing problem. Mass-production of housing is limited not by the excessive durability of existing houses, but by the fact that average incomes are too low to enable the ordinary consumer to buy a house at existing prices. The likelihood is overwhelmingly that if a firm could introduce a method of building which would result in a substantial reduction in the price of houses and flats, it could find a mass market quite irrespective of the durability of existing houses or the durability of the new cheaper houses it was putting on the market.

None of these complicating factors, therefore, provides any convincing case for artificially reducing the economic life of consumer durables, or provides any argument against consumer countermeasures designed to extend product life.

4. *After-sales service*

In the classic case of fashion change, women's clothes, the problems of after-sales service do not arise and it may be assumed that economies of large-scale production, though they exist (as evidenced by the well-known multiple stores) can be achieved by relatively small producers. With consumers' mechanical equipment the case is different. There is very convincing evidence that rapid (*e.g.*, annual) model changes make it difficult for retailers to maintain adequate stocks of spare parts and may also demand higher technical skill on the part of repairers. Model changes are only one of the factors affecting efficient repair services; others are the general low level of skill in retailing and the fact that consumer ignorance, which in this case it would not be practicable or reasonable to try to dissipate, makes for an easy life for inefficient servicers.

In a test on garage repair services the Consumers' Association[7] inserted four faults into some cars and took them for repair to eight garages in the London area. The results were:

---

[7] From the October 1966 issue of *Motoring Which?*, by permission of the publishers, Consumers' Association, 14 Buckingham Street, London, W.C.2.

Garage No. 1 remedied all four faults.

Nos. 2, 3, and 4 remedied only two of the faults.

5 All the faults were dealt with.

6 Three of the four faults were dealt with, but more work than necessary was carried out.

7 Two of the four faults were put right.

8 Three of the four faults were put right.

Motoring Which? commented:

> Our exercise shows, as numerous people have shown before, that if you take a few cars to a few garages where they have never been seen before, you will get widely different treatment at widely different prices. . . . Perhaps the most noticeable thing is that the two garages which did the best job also charged the least—a garage which can diagnose faults quickly and accurately will not waste their time and your money. Our exercise also shows that when in doubt some garages replaced components when adjustments would have been sufficient, or sometimes even when a component was in perfect order.

This indication that the competence of repair services for consumer durables is doubtful is supported by several other investigations which have been carried out by consumer groups and other organizations in Britain, and by the Consumers' Union in the U.S.A. (See, for example, *Consumer Reports*, October 1964, pages 462–463.) Tests on garages and television repair services made by *Shopper's Guide* in 1961 showed an even worse situation than did the C.A.'s tests; if these two are in any way representative there seems to have been an improvement in repair services in the intervening years.

5. *Avenues of escape*

There is not much doubt that, in the absence of institutional countermeasures, manufacturers will find it in their own interest to persuade consumers to accept as high a rate of fashion obsolescence as they can. The question is what remedies are available.

As always, at the head of the list must come more consumer research and consumer education. The type of research carried out by Messrs Fisher, Griliches, and Kaysen should, as a matter of urgency, be refined and extended to all industries subject to fashion changes. Given full consumer knowledge, especially of the effect of fashion and model changes on prices—and their effect on repair servicing and spare parts supply where complex items of consumer equipment are concerned—the trend towards more rapid obsolescence would be slowed down.[8]

The second major study should be the comparative life of producer goods and roughly similar consumer goods. The earliest comprehensive work on consumer protection, Stuart Chase and F. J. Schlink, *Your Money's Worth*, is mainly devoted to the lessons which can be learned by or on behalf of consumers from government purchasing experience of such things as military uniforms, soap, cleaning equipment, housing and furniture, and so on. For all the items of which the government is a large-scale purchaser, precise standards are drawn up and enforced, and the resulting purchase is generally greatly superior and at the same time much cheaper than its civilian equivalent. One example among many cited by Chase and Schlink was that of a door hinge for government use tested by the U.S. Bureau of Standards, which was found to have a life fifty times that of similarly priced products on sale to private consumers. In the durable-goods field, practically identical goods are bought by individual consumers and by large-scale purchasers such as hotels and catering establishments (refrigerators), launderettes (washing machines), television and car-hire firms, and others. Detailed technical and economic studies of the differences and the reasons for them in these purchases would provide the best possible starting-point for recommendations as to how standards of goods bought by the final consumer could be improved.

Utilization on behalf of the final consumer of standards and grades originally derived with the needs of intermediate consumers in mind was stressed in the late President Kennedy's message to Congress on consumer protection in March 1962.

---

[8] One authority claims to detect in the U.S.A. a trend already towards rationality in design of consumer durable goods. "Automobile styles, gaudy with chrome, tail fins and fancy grille work a few years ago, are yielding to simple, unadorned lines as more attention is focused on comfort, safety and general utility. Changes in clothing styles, though gradual and at times retrogressive, also show a trend towards simplicity and utility. The same trend is evident, and will become more so, in buildings and homes. New materials, produceable in abundance, will lend themselves to applications where simplicity and utility will not detract from beauty and good taste. Durability will not preclude economy in original cost, yet variety and flexibility will permit change at a reasonable cost." E. Finlay Carter (of Stanford Research Institute, California) writing on "Domestic Life in 1984" in the *New Scientist*, April 2nd, 1964. In my view this prognosis contains an element of wishful thinking.

Too little has been done to make available to consumers the results of pertinent government research . . . Many [government] agencies are concerned—as aids to those principally concerned with their activities, in co-operation with industry or for federal procurement programmes—in testing the performance of certain products, developing standards and specifications and assembling a wide range of related information which would be of immense use to consumers and to consumer organizations. The beneficial results of these efforts—in the Departments of Agriculture, Commerce, Defence, and Health, Education and Welfare, and in the General Services Administration and other agencies—should be more widely publicized. This is but one part of a wider problem—the failure of governmental agencies to assist specific consideration of the consumer's needs and point of view.

President Kennedy proposed (in addition to forming a Consumer Advisory Council to the President's Council of Economic Advisors) to establish in each federal-government agency which might have a bearing on consumer matters a specialist on consumer affairs. This is not really useful. What is needed is a research organization, or research department, with the requisite resources and technical knowledge to study specifications devised for government (or industrial and commercial) use and to see when and how they could be of use to consumers.[9]

Apart from research and education, what institutional changes could be brought about to induce producers to extend the life of durable goods; more specifically, what financial incentives and sanctions could be brought to bear on them to this end?

(1) A start, although a weak one, is to be found in the manufacturer's guarantee. At present a guarantee normally covers two years, is subject to many variations on questions such as who is to pay for transport costs and labour charges on the defective article, and the decision on any disputed point in the guarantee usually rests with the manufacturer. (More important at present is the fact that many guarantees as at present framed exclude all other warranties "express or implied" and thus *reduce* the consumer's right under the Sale of Goods Act and at common law. (It may be assumed, however,

[9] Comparisons of this sort need not of course be confined to durable goods. The annual report of the Scientific Adviser to the London County Council for 1962 reported that nearly three-quarters of a million gallons of paint a year are used by the Council, and its paint section tested 66,463 samples during the year. More than half of the brands tested were rejected; a detailed statistical breakdown of the reasons for the rejection (but not the names of the brands) is given in the report.

that these "exclusion clauses" will generally be dropped in the near future, owing to the amount of criticism they have attracted.) In any case, two years is quite inadequate for a complex piece of domestic equipment, which could reasonably be expected to have a life of ten or fifteen years. There seems no good reason why legal liability for a durable good should not cover, say, five years; if this were done manufacturers would be forced to insure against losses due to defective goods and the formidable resources of the insurance companies might be brought to bear on them to induce them to devote more attention to durability and to improve quality control.[10] In France under the *agrément* system, architects and engineers are legally responsible for their buildings for ten or twelve years after completion. They therefore insist on testing of materials and components; the *agrément* is the certificate of test. Such testing is insisted upon by the insurance companies (as a result of being legally responsible, architects and engineers insure themselves against defects in their buildings).

(2) The interests of sellers of second-hand durables is evidently to keep the price as high as possible, and this might be used to offset over-rapid depreciation. In September 1964 the British firm Standard-Triumph International announced that the Triumph-Herald range of cars, introduced in 1959, would continue in production for at least another five years. The motive apparently was to reassure buyers of new cars that the second-hand value would not suffer a severe fall. The interests of the hire-purchase companies are also involved in maintaining the value of the second-hand article, if they have to take repossession of an article, but they do not in the past seem to have been induced to take any positive steps in this direction, and their dependence on the second-hand market is considerably reduced by the 1964 Hire Purchase Act.

[10] It is a subject for investigation and consideration why the insurance companies are not more active in all fields in putting pressure on those whom they insure to protect themselves against the risks insured against. For example, it is possible to insure against fire and burglary but the insurance companies do very little to see that those insured take reasonable precautions against fire and burglary. It may be that the cost of enforcing such provisions would be higher than the cost at present incurred in making payments to the fire-stricken and the burgled, in which case little could be done; or it may be that competition among the insurance companies prevents premiums being raised to the level needed for enforcement, in which case there might be grounds for government intervention.

(3) Some of the present trouble is grounded in the fact that retailers, who under the Sale of Goods Act, 1893, and Roman Law from which it is derived, are legally responsible for ensuring that goods sold are "fit for the purpose required" and "of merchantable quality" (phrases which appear to mean the same thing), frequently have not the technical knowledge or the equipment to carry out repairs and servicing efficiently. Here is one reason for the growth of manufacturers' guarantees. In the U.S.A. "discount houses" have flourished on the principle that prices to the consumer can be markedly reduced if the retailer provides no services of any sort (including delivery and after-sales service) and the customer has to rely entirely on the manufacturer for servicing. It seems safe to assume that this trend will manifest itself in other countries. Its legal implications are to some extent obvious but cannot be dealt with in detail here.

Another probable line of advance, already evident in the U.S.A., is the establishment of specialist service and repair organizations divorced from retailing. Indeed, it is surprising that large commercial organizations (retailer, manufacturer, or neither) have not yet entered the repairs field on any appreciable scale, since the small or one-man organizations which do the bulk of repair work are manifestly inadequate, and an organization providing good service would therefore be likely to prosper. (It is not by this intended to imply that there is no place for small organizations in the field of servicing.) The explanation is probably in part the high rate of obsolescence which consumers have been persuaded or forced to accept as normal.

(4) A possibility which has not been explored to any extent is that of building a consumer durable good in replaceable prefabricated component parts, so that the consumer could without difficulty detach and replace the failed part without buying a whole new product. The object of such a solution would be to allow the unskilled consumer to carry out the replacement. It would only be satisfactory if the "component sets" were sufficiently small for the consumer not to have to replace numbers of components unnecessarily. At present it can only be suggested as a subject deserving of technical study.

(5) A more radical approach is for the manufacturer to offer a complete service, the initial charge including maintenance over the whole life of the product. This is done in the United States by the American Telephone and Telegraph Company and to a lesser extent

by other companies (notably International Business Machines, General Electric, the Radio Corporation of America, and the Ford Company). In some cases, the item may be provided under a lease arrangement which incorporates complete servicing during the period of the agreement. In others, the manufacturer may offer a maintenance contract on an optional basis at an extra charge. In Britain, the consumer products division of Standard Telephones and Cables has introduced a plan identical with the "contract mainten-ance" scheme for television purchase which incorporates re-payments, maintenance, and insurance in a single agreement, for customers who wish to buy rather than rent certain types of television-set. On payment of a deposit, the customer becomes the owner of the set and receives full maintenance and insurance over a three-year period, together with the option of further maintenance at special rates for an indefinite period. At the beginning of the year, the dealer is paid a fixed labour fee by S.T.C. for the maintenance of each receiver sold. "The dealer will therefore make doubly sure that, should he have to service a set, a return visit will be unneces-sary", according to the S.T.C. spokesman.[11] Certainly any system whereby either the manufacturer or retailer receives a fixed payment for repairs, either initially or periodically, increases considerably the incentive to make the equipment as efficient as possible at the outset, to design it so that it will need only the minimum of repairs, and to ensure that a repair, when carried out, is efficient and complete. "Contract maintenance" for a house and all its major pieces of equipment might, indeed, eventually provide the solution for the problem of obsolescence.

(6) Renting rather than buying has similar advantages though it does not allow the consumer the advantage of eventual cessation of payments. Television-sets, and to a lesser extent gas and electric cookers, are rented on a considerable scale. In such cases the lessor (the TV rental company, or the gas or electricity board) has to take the necessary measures to see that the item is durable and needs a minimum of maintenance and expenditure. There has been a spec-tacular growth in renting of television-sets in the U.K.[12] In mid-1964 there were 13·5 million sets in use, of which one-third were rented, compared with a quarter three years earlier. More than 50 per cent

[11] Quoted in *The Financial Times*, February 21st, 1964.
[12] Most of the information in this paragraph is from an article in the Econo-mist Intelligence Unit's *Retail Business*, July 1964, "The rental of consumer durables."

of new deliveries of television-sets since 1962 were for renting. Two surveys, one by *Which?* and the other by the *Evening News*, have shown that overwhelmingly the main reason for renting rather than buying of television-sets is the service problem. Renters can rely on free repairs and better and quicker service, including Sundays and Bank Holidays—though the possibility of colour TV making bought sets obsolete, and government restrictions on hire purchase, have also aided the growth of renting. Outside television, the most important rented item is cookers, where about 16 per cent of those in use are rented from gas and electricity boards (80 per cent of rented cookers are in council houses). Only 6 per cent of refrigerators in use in the U.K. are rented, only 2 per cent of washing machines, and 1 per cent of radios. A factor in the low rental proportion in these latter two items may be the smaller degree of servicing required compared with television-sets and refrigerators.

These proposals would have the effect of putting increased pressure on manufacturers to pay more attention to physical durability and quality control. To a large extent, they leave un-affected the problem of the annual model change. This is prob-ably the more important aspect and certainly the most difficult to tackle.

The vulnerability of consumers to producer-inspired fashion changes lies mainly in the fact that producers, by acting in concert, can give the impression that the change is autonomous and not in-spired. Indeed, regular fashion changes have now become so much a feature of the women's clothing industry that it would be difficult to distinguish cause and effect (we are not here discussing long-term trends—*e.g.*, Victorian, 1920's, and 1930's clothing styles, but annual changes). In other industries, however, the trend could be nipped in the bud.

Concerted changes of fashion by agreement among manufacturers should be classified as a restrictive practice and should become illegal. As an example, let us revert to the U.S. car industry. It appears unlikely that a genuine fashion change (still less, of course, a technological improvement) should be revealed to each manu-facturer every year in the same month of the year, and this case is clearly the archetype of the pure or "induced" fashion change. In the main, as numerous observers have noted, the changes in a par-ticular year are minor, concerning colour and extraneous design features; real technological advances appear at the most only about every five years. If the real cost of such changes were proved to be high (as, on the available evidence, it is) it could be made illegal for manufacturers to agree to introduce a new model change simultaneously, just as it is illegal for them to agree to raise prices. This would have the effect of obliterating clear distinctions between "this year's" and "last year's" models and would, probably, break the back of rapid producer-inspired model changes.

11

The New Just Price

> Joanna Wilkinson, aged 9, of Nottingham complained to her
> M.P. when the cost of marbles at the local shop went up by
> 1*d*. to sevenpence. Mr Michael English (Labour, Nottingham
> West) took up the case with the Board of Trade and after a
> full investigation Joanna has had her penny refunded and the
> cost of marbles has been adjusted. Joanna . . . told her M.P.
> that she thought sixpence was enough to pay for a packet of
> marbles. Mr English found that the shopkeeper was only pass-
> ing on a price increase he had to pay when making the
> purchase.
>
> *The Guardian*, April 25th, 1967

The first attempt after the war to prevent prices and wages from
rising in conditions of full employment, under Sir Stafford Cripps,
was directed mainly to wages, as there was a comprehensive system
of price control already in being. The attempt broke down in September 1950 when, following price increases caused by devaluation
and rearmament, the General Council of the T.U.C.'s proposals for
a renewal of wage restraint were defeated. Between 1951 and 1961
restraint of prices and wages was regarded as a purely macro-
economic question, and it was in any case doubtful whether the trade
unions would co-operate fully with a Conservative government in
any attempt to restrain wages. The Council on Prices, Productivity,
and Incomes, set up in 1957, was never intended to be more than
advisory and its reports had no perceptible effects and was disbanded
after four years.

In 1962 the newly created National Economic Development Council succeeded in getting the T.U.C. to participate in discussions of
means of linking stabilization policy and measures to speed up
economic growth. In the same year the National Incomes Commission was set up, stipulating a range of permissible wage increases of
between 2 and 2½ per cent and increasing this to 3–3½ per cent in
line with the growth target adopted by the N.E.D.C.

After the Labour government came into power in October 1964

a Joint Statement of Intent on Productivity, Prices, and Incomes was issued (on December 16th, 1964) by representatives of the government, the employers' organizations, and the T.U.C. which declared: "We must take urgent and vigorous action (i) to raise productivity throughout industry and commerce; (ii) to keep increases in total money incomes in line with increases in national output; (iii) to maintain a stable price level." It was agreed to set up machinery to keep under review the general movement of prices and of all money incomes; and "to examine particular cases in order to advise whether or not the behaviour of prices or of wages, salaries or other money incomes is in the national interest as defined by the government after consultation with management and unions." The National Economic Development Council was invited to carry out the first of these two functions; the National Board for Prices and Incomes was set up to carry out the second, the investigation of particular cases of prices and incomes behaviour.

The way in which the Board was to operate was set out in a White Paper, *The Machinery of Prices and Incomes Policy* (Cmnd. 2577), and the criteria by which price and wage increases were to be judged were set out in another White Paper, *Prices and Incomes Policy*, (Cmnd. 2639), published in February and April 1965 respectively. The former states (para II): "In principle, the Prices Review Division will be able to investigate any price or group of prices (manufacturing, wholesale or retail) of goods and services in private industry and in nationalized industry. Both particular cases of price change and cases in which there has been no change, although prima facie some reduction appears to be warranted, will be covered."

The conditions which an enterprise has to satisfy before it can raise its prices are set out in paragraph 9 of the April 1965 White Paper:

(i) if output per employee cannot be increased sufficiently to allow wages and salaries to increase at a rate consistent with the criteria for incomes stated in paragraph 15 below without some increase in prices, and no offsetting reductions can be made in non-labour costs per unit of output or in the return sought on investment;

(ii) if there are unavoidable increases in non-labour costs such as materials, fuel, services or marketing costs per unit of output which cannot be offset by reductions in labour or capital costs per unit of output or in the return sought on investment;

(iii) if there are unavoidable increases in capital costs per unit of output which cannot be offset by reductions in non-capital costs per unit of output or in the return sought on investment;

(iv) if, after every effort has been made to reduce costs, the enterprise has been unable to secure the capital required to meet home and overseas demand.

Paragraph 15, giving the criteria for incomes increases of above the norm, states that exceptional pay rises should be confined to circumstances where the employees concerned "by accepting more exacting work or a major change in working practices" make a direct contribution towards increasing productivity; ("even in such cases some of the benefit should accrue to the community as a whole in the form of lower prices"); where it is essential in the national interest to secure a change in the distribution of manpower and a pay increase would be both necessary and effective for that purpose; and where wage and salary levels are too low to maintain a reasonable standard of living.

When the Prices and Incomes Board had been at work for just over a year, a severe deterioration in the balance of payments led to the "July measures" of 1966, aiming at a complete stop on all non-essential wage and price increases, up to the end of 1966, followed by six months of severe restraint. On prices, the standstill was to apply "except to the limited extent that increases in prices or charges may be necessary because of marked increases which cannot be absorbed, in costs of imported materials, or which arise from changes in supply for seasonal or other reasons, or which are due to action by the government such as increased taxation." (*Prices and Incomes Standstill*, Cmnd. 3073, July 1966, para. 4). The incomes norm during the six-month standstill was to be regarded as zero.

In March 1967 a further White Paper was issued on *Prices and Incomes Policy after 30th June 1967* (Cmnd. 3235) indicating a somewhat less rigid policy than that followed during the six months' standstill and six months' severe restraint, but nevertheless rather more rigid than prevailed before July 1966.[1] The criteria of

---

[1] Commenting on the success of the prices and incomes policy to that date, the White Paper remarked: "The July measures have had considerable success. Exports have been advancing strongly and the trade gap has been narrowed. . . . Sterling has been greatly strengthened and the gain to the reserves has made it possible to repay a satisfactory amount of short-term debt. Internally, the measures have eliminated the excess pressure of demand, have freed resources for export production and other essential purposes, and have slowed down the rise in prices and incomes." (Para. 2). Devaluation followed eight months later.

"unavoidable" increases in labour, capital, or other costs were re-iterated for price increases, and the same criteria as in Cmnd. 2639 for wage increases—held to be justifiable if there is an increase in labour productivity attributable to action by workers (but even in these cases some benefit should accrue to the community as a whole in the form of lower prices); if wage increases are essential to secure changes in the distribution of manpower; and in the case of low-paid workers. The selection of prices for investigation by the P.I.B. is elucidated as follows (para. 7): "It would not be in the interests of economic efficiency to seek to operate the policy in a rigid form involving a very widespread and detailed supervision of individual prices . . . the aim will be to concentrate on those prices which are of economic significance, including those of importance in the cost of living."

Up to the end of March 1968, the Prices and Incomes Board had published sixty-eight reports, twenty-nine dealing with incomes, and in addition some reports covering both incomes and prices in particular industries (*e.g.*, Report No. 2, *Wages, Costs and Prices in the Printing Industry*), some general reports (*e.g.*, No. 36, *Productivity Agreements* and No. 23, *Productivity and Pay During the Period of Severe Restraint*), as well as its own annual reports.

The Board has frequently found itself acting as unpaid efficiency consultant to the industry or organization in question. It suggested after examining coal distribution costs[2] that rail transport costs could be reduced by dispatching fully loaded trains to destinations capable of receiving large quantities; mechanization of depots; and rationalization of collecting, ordering, and delivering by coal merchants. The Board also examined pithead prices of coal[3] and suggested that production should be concentrated as quickly as possible in the most profitable pit areas (perhaps not very helpfully, as the National Coal Board has been trying to do so for many years) and that time-rates should be substituted for the existing system of piece-rate earnings.

In its report on Road Haulage Charges a number of proposals were made, including the extension of shift working, adoption of a more flexible working week, and of schedules related to the 40 m.p.h. speed limit, and the use of recording devices to measure times actually travelled.

The G.P.O. was recommended to make more use of part-time

2 Report No. 21, Cmnd, 3094, September 1966.
3 Report No. 12, Cmnd. 2919, December 1965.

workers in areas of labour shortage, to reduce overtime working, to carry out a selective marketing campaign to promote sales of telephones in areas where existing capacity is under-utilized, and to abolish or obtain a governmental subsidy for the telegram service.[4] The latter has been retained by the G.P.O. on social grounds, but the Prices and Incomes Board discovered that urgent "life and death" telegrams now comprise only 1 per cent of all telegrams.

Rather less specific recommendations were made for the laundry and dry-cleaning trades.[5] "As far as the laundry industry is concerned we consider that a major contribution to the absorption of wage increases can come only from further amalgamations", which would lead to closure of some establishments and fuller utilization of others; the use of labour-saving equipment; and rationalization of delivery services (i.e., payment by customers who wanted delivery). The Board concluded that in dry-cleaning the ability of the trade to absorb rising costs had been reduced by "a more rapid growth of 'unit shops' than the expansion of the total business justified", and recommended that the trade organization should offer advice (presumably discouraging) to potential entrants to the industry. "For the rest, though competition is often in service rather than price, we consider more price competition, particularly by the larger firms, could help to reduce over-capacity." The Board did not indicate any way in which price competition might be increased, nor did it discuss its criterion for the right number of dry-cleaning shops.

Reporting on Bank Charges[6] the P.I.B. criticized the agreement between the major banks on rates of interest paid on deposits.

We consider that this agreement has led to a loss in their power to attract deposits, to a loss therefore in their power to extend and diversify their lending activities, to an inability to secure to a larger extent the economies of scale which could follow on such an extension—in short, to a loss in their relative place in the entire financial system. A recovery of place for the banks requires in our view a greater degree of competition between the banks themselves for deposits and therefore between the banks as a whole and other financial institutions.

[4] No. 58, *Post Office Charges*, Cmnd. 3574, March 1968.

[5] No. 20, *Laundry and Dry Cleaning Charges*, Cmnd. 3093, September 1966.

[6] Report No. 34, Cmnd. 3292, May 1967.

M

On Costs and Charges in the Radio and Television Rental and Relay Industry[7] the Board concluded:

> It would be easier for customers to inform themselves if suppliers were to include in their advertisements a statement of the charges payable over a period of three years. Powers to require this could be taken in the Consumer Protection Bill; though, in the end, more information can only improve matters if customers are prepared to look for the cheapest contract that meets their needs.

When the Board has not been able to put forward positive recommendations of this kind its reports have been less helpful. Some of its reports after September 1966 were concerned with whether price increases in the retail or wholesale trades were "justified" following the imposition of the Selective Employment Tax. It undertook the same task following devaluation of the pound in November 1967 to see whether certain industries were making larger increases in prices than was justified by the proportionate increase in their raw materials prices. Most of the post-devaluation price increases were approved, but in its report on the *Distribution Costs of Fresh Fruit and Vegetables*[8] the P.I.B. recommended that an increase of 2*d*. in the £ proposed by the National Federation of Fruit and Potato Trades for wholesale prices should be withdrawn, on the grounds that "unit labour costs in relation to turnover vary greatly from firm to firm and indeed from season to season."

In a number of other cases the P.I.B. has confined itself to reporting on whether the actual or proposed price increases are "justified" by (or, more accurately, statistically disproportionate to) the rise in costs. On prices of household and toilet soap, soap powders, and synthetic detergents, it concluded that "the increase in the prices of soap powders was justified by the sharp increase in costs. . . . The increase in the price of synthetic powders was greater than justified by the indicated movement in the costs." In some other cases, the rise in costs has been considered in conjunction with the need of the industry to maintain or increase investment, and the Board here emerges into much more debatable territory. In its report on Compound Fertilizers it was concluded that owing to cost increases and increased competition in the domestic market "profits have been declining and are now so low that without a price increase the industry's capacity to invest will be adversely affected." A price

[7] Report No. 52, Cmnd. 3520, January 1968.
[8] Report No. 31, Cmnd. 3265, April 1967.

increase in newsprint was considered to be justified during the period of severe restraint owing to increases in the cost of imported raw materials and the need for finance to cover new investment.

However, once the criterion of finance to cover new investment is incorporated, a number of far-reaching questions are introduced. If prices are raised now to cover investment costs will it be possible to reduce them at some date in the future, and if not will future demand be adversely affected? (If the answer to the latter question is no, the even more pressing question arises of should it not be?) Is the "need for new investment" based on the assumption that the industry should continue to supply a fixed percentage of the home market, and might it not be desirable, if costs cannot be reduced, to increase imports? (Fertilizers are an industry which in Britain is protected by exceptionally high tariffs.) If an increase in imports is not predictable or desirable might not an investigation be made into how costs and prices in the home industry compare with those prevailing in other countries, particularly where, as with post-office charges and electricity, the industry is an effective monopoly?

A discussion of the work of the Prices and Incomes Board in regard to wages and other incomes would involve the complex and controversial questions connected with incomes policy, and will not be attempted. The work of the Board in relation to prices may, however, be assessed in the light of conclusions reached in earlier parts of the book.

In Chapter 3, it was noted that the mark of a price "artificially" held below equilibrium price was the creation of shortages. The P.I.B., evidently, has not created shortages of the products whose prices have been examined, though in one case, bread, it came near doing so temporarily when it decided that a price increase would be unjustified. Strikes in the industry followed in the autumn of 1965 after employers refused wage increases. There are two explanations, both of which have applied in the period 1965 to 1968. The first is that holding prices below equilibrium *in a period of unemployment and demand deflation* will not necessarily lead to shortages (see Chapter 4, section on "Administered prices"). Factors of production will not then leave the industry in question as they are less likely to be able to find employment elsewhere, and profits and wages may be successfully held down. The second explanation is that the P.I.B. has, in most cases where it has recommended that a price increase should not take place, also pointed out how costs can be kept down (*i.e.*, how the supply curve can be shifted to the right). A third possible explanation, of course, is that the recommendations of the P.I.B. on prices have had only a negligible effect.

If the P.I.B. is not open to the criticism that its actions have created shortages, it may be open to criticism similar to those which can be made of price control in other respects, particularly in regard to the selection of commodities for control. The White Paper *Prices and Incomes Policy: an Early Warning System* (Cmnd. 2808, November 1965) discussed this problem and concluded:

> Although the agreed policy for prices and incomes applies with equal force to all who are responsible for determining prices and charges, it is neither necessary nor practicable to have "early warning" of each of the very large number of individual price changes which are liable to occur in the course of a year. In general, the aim must be to include goods and services which are of particular economic significance or consumer goods which are important elements in the cost of living. In drawing up a list, however, it is necessary to have regard to factors which make inclusion of particular items unsuitable. Examples of these are goods the prices of which are determined by very short-term supply and demand factors or mainly by the cost of imported materials. . . . The consumer goods to be included should be of general consumer interest and reasonably representative of this class of goods; they should also present fewer difficulties of administration than other items which have been considered. For example, some goods such as clothing present great difficulties because the product is both varied and continually changing or because a large number of small firms are involved.

This list excludes a very large area of consumer expenditure: non-manufactured foods, because of the variability of prices; clothing, because of the large number of firms; consumer durable goods, because of variability of quality; the building industry, because of the large number of firms and local price variations; land prices, because of variations and lack of information; and retail and service trades, except where recommended or otherwise uniform prices exist. What is left are standardized goods produced by oligopolistic industries (such as flour, soap and detergents, cement), or the prices of utilities and nationalized industries. (It was, incidentally, only after a major political storm over electricity price increases in 1967 that the latter were referred to the Prices and Incomes Board, which does not select its own subjects for investigation but has them referred to it by the government.) The procedure is subject to even more severe difficulties as regards *enforcement* than is legal price control—indeed, as there is no enforcement, it will not be known whether the recommendations of the P.I.B. have had any effect in individual cases unless it carries out a second investigation for this purpose.

The psychological effect of investigations of particular prices, and the effect on industries not being investigated, has to be taken into account. Certainly anything which disrupts the semi-automatic process of passing on cost increases in prices, and which induces firms to examine their efficiency more closely, is a good thing. That the selection of industries for examination is arbitrary (prices in some industries are easy to investigate, in other industries almost impossible) is not necessarily a very serious condemnation. Nor is the fact that the Board's only sanction may lie in publicity.

In the last resort, "prices and incomes policies" have to be judged by whether they have any effect in moderating the rate of increase of prices. The Prices and Incomes Board in Britain has so far been working almost entirely in a period when excess demand was non-existent, due to deflationary budgetary and monetary policies. A definitive conclusion will be possible only when a prices and incomes policy has operated in different conditions. While it is at present impossible to say categorically what the effect of such policies has been, it has not been large. As far as incomes are concerned, the National Institute of Economic and Social Research has calculated[9] that in the period 1965 to 1968, except during the complete freeze in the latter half of 1966, the rate of increase in wages was almost the same as would have been expected from the degree of unemployment. Incomes rose as much as they would have done if no incomes policy had been in force. In its third annual report the P.I.B. itself made an attempt to estimate the effect of its policies.[10] The conclusion was that in the years *1965 and 1966* the prices and incomes policy reduced the rate of increase of *incomes* by rather less than 1 per cent a year. This in itself would constitute quite a significant achievement, but as pointed out by the N.I.E.S.R. it seems that wage rises which would otherwise have been awarded during

[9] N.I.E.S.R. *Economic Review*, February 1968, p. 26: "During the short period of freeze itself, there is no doubt that there was an effect. Both the wage rates index and the earnings levelled off for about six months. The question to be decided here is whether or not there was any permanent effect, or whether the freeze simply postponed the increases. . . . It looks rather as if it was simply a postponement."

[10] Third General Report of the National Board for Prices and Incomes, Cmnd. 3715. July 1968, p. 67.

the complete freeze of July–December 1966 were merely postponed, and incomes caught up in 1967. On prices, the P.I.B. estimated that in 1965 and 1966 they rose *more* than might have been expected. Definitive conclusions can, of course, be put forward only when the prices and incomes policy has been operated for several more years.

12

Conclusion

> If there is going to be a free-for-all, we are part of the all.
> FRANK COUSINS,
> General Secretary, Transport and General Workers' Union

In the course of analysing some consumer problems in the preceding chapters, we have put forward suggestions as to how they might be dealt with in a fully consumer-orientated economy. Probably it would be futile to attempt a summary of these discussions, many of which are themselves only summaries. Before concluding, it seems worth while, however, to attempt some further elucidation of the main sphere in which modern economies have failed consumers, their inability to prevent the general price level from rising.

Perhaps the most popular explanation of the inflationary process is that which attributes it initially to wage claims by trade unions, leading to higher costs for businesses, leading to higher prices, and in turn to more wage claims. This picture is not generally approved of by economists, who prefer to look at things in terms of total demand and total supply. The "trade union pressure" view of inflation does not explain why or under what conditions a wage claim is likely to be successful. And if a firm is able to raise its prices to recoup the expense of higher wages, why could it not do so before?

But there are also compelling arguments on the other side. If the economy worked as micro-economic theory suggests it should, then in the absence of "overall" excess demand no workers should ever get higher wages unless there is a shortage of labour in their industry, or in consequence of a productivity agreement. (The scope for the latter, incidentally, is much more limited than is sometimes realized.) In times of moderately heavy unemployment, such as in 1966–68, hardly any workers should get pay rises. In practice, the economy obviously does not work this way.

It is not possible to settle definitively here the continuing debate between macro-economic and micro-economic explanations of inflation. And, to some extent, in economics as in medicine, the search for definitive causes is fruitless. All we need to know in practice is how inflation is to be stopped. Here the supporters of prices and incomes policies are on strong ground. Prices and wages since the war have continued to rise even at times of high unemployment and excess capacity. To put the same point in a different fashion, if every time there were a rise in the retail price index, further overall deflationary measures were taken, the degree of unemployment and the loss of production would be enormous.

Trying to find points of agreement rather than disagreement: there is a concensus of opinion that the *main* burden of the task of preventing prices from rising must lie with fiscal and monetary policy. The role of micro-economic measures is essentially supplementary. Neither, probably, is there much disagreement that government investigatory bodies such as the Prices and Incomes Board can play a useful part over a much wider field than is usually subsumed under the heading of "monopoly policy", which may nevertheless be described as intended to remove market imperfections. The wage-price guideposts inaugurated in the U.S.A. in 1962 have focused attention

on the way in which particular markets behave, and [they] bring into relief institutional arrangements which make prices higher than necessary. They helped to reduce restriction on oil imports, and to stimulate a new plan for government-sponsored efforts to reduce costs in construction. They may well re-enforce efforts to do something about training requirements and conditions for qualification in the medical profession. They may impinge on the role of the Civil Aeronautics Board in determining airline fares. They came close to stimulating new legislation on the right to strike in connection with the airline dispute. They force the government to choose strategic points of action to restrain prices, and thereby foster continuous questioning of a series of relationships that might otherwise be taken for granted.[1]

This line of approach, it may be observed, is very different from that which is sometimes thought to be the focal-point of prices and incomes policies: the laying down of annual guideposts or norms for incomes increases during a given year, based on the expected increase in national output during the year, coupled with examination

[1] J. Sheahan, *The wage-price guideposts* (the Brookings Institution, Washington, 1967), p. 171.

of particular price and wage increases to see whether they are "justified".

The announcement of a norm of a specified amount (say, 3 per cent) for wage increases during a certain year will mean that few workers will be satisfied with less. Further, pre-determined norms raise problems of a logical as well as of a practical or economic character. When workers in a particular industry are negotiating for a pay rise, if the "norm" is to be observed the decision on whether to grant the claim or not must depend on the outcome of all other pay negotiations taking place during the year in question. But the outcome of many of these cannot in fact be known.

Examining particular price and wage claims to determine whether or not they are "justified" raises difficulties almost as severe. In a multi-product firm the allocation of overhead costs between different products is bound to be arbitrary and any one allocation is open to dispute. In assessing profit levels, relating profits to capital employed raises serious practical problems. Many other questions turn on matters of judgment, and there may be no way of saying until after the event whether a price increase was justified. Thus a firm might need to make large profits for a temporary period to finance new investment—a criterion which, as suggested in the preceding chapter, seems on occasion to have been rather uncritically accepted by the Prices and Incomes Board. It might be better to accept the "need for new investment" argument only if the firm or industry concerned gave a guarantee that prices would be reduced after the investment had been completed, specifying the time and amount of the reduction.

An increase in demand "justifies" an increase in prices as a means of calling forth a larger supply, and an anticipated increase in future demand may justify higher profits to finance new investment. However, unless the firm in question has a near-absolute monopoly, a rise in price for this purpose is itself likely to affect demand adversely, so that a price increase cannot be regarded as justified on this criterion without an examination of probable future demand, supply, and price trends in competing firms and industries.

If it were feasible to decide what constitutes a fair profit it would then be necessary to decide what level of costs is "justified", an even more tortuous matter. As profits do not normally account for more than 10 per cent of sales value, if our concern is to keep down prices the problem resolves itself into 90 per cent one of cost reduction and 10 per cent one of profit reduction. A particular level of costs can be said to be justified, if at all, only after extremely complex inter-firm and perhaps international comparisons.

When a question raises difficulties as far-reaching as these it is usually safe—or at least wise—to assume that the question which is being asked is the wrong one, and that it would be better to ask a different question. As it is very difficult to distinguish justified from unjustified price increases, perhaps we ought to start from the assumption that nearly all price increases are equally deplorable. What we need to know is not which price increases are justified and which are not, but how to mitigate or prevent any price increase. If so, the question to be asked is not "Is it justifiable?" but "Is it avoidable?" In addition, in many cases there are much larger potential gains to be derived from comparing existing prices than from examining price increases.

The electricity industry may be cited as an example of the difficulties in examining price increases to see whether they are justified, and at the same time to indicate the possibilities of a wider and more pragmatic approach. Since 1959 coal and electricity prices have been rising more rapidly than gas and oil prices, and there is not much doubt that these trends will continue. After the 1961 White Paper on the *Financial and Economic Obligations of the Nationalized Industries* (mentioned in Chapter 8) it became accepted that the electricity industry should rely more on self-financing rather than borrowing, and the industry accordingly raised its price to cover part of the cost of its huge investment programme—by far the largest of any industry and making the capital expenditure of even oil-refining or car-manufacturing look small by comparison.

An investigating economist would certainly conclude that the trend of prices in the electricity industry was justified, though he might have minor reservations about the precise degree of self-financing which is needed, the target rate of return on capital to be aimed at, or whether the industry should move further towards marginal cost pricing, by raising its peak prices more than it has done. But adopting a pragmatic rather than an *a priori* approach, there *are* alternatives open to the industrial and private consumer of fuel, and from this standpoint the electricity industry stands doubly condemned, not only for raising prices but also for pre-empting a very large slice of the nation's limited capital resources. Any practicable measures should be taken to induce consumers to switch their consumption away from electricity to other fuels, faster than the change in relative prices itself will induce them to do. What measures could be taken to this end could be spelt out only after a detailed technical and economic study of *all* the fuel industries. A few of them—ensuring that new houses are not connected only to the electricity supply, devoting scientific research to finding substitutes for electricity for non-fuel energy purposes—have been mentioned (Chapter 3 and Chapter 8).

Incomes, not prices, are usually regarded as the central point of a prices and incomes policy. While it is impossible to discuss incomes policy fully in a book mainly devoted to prices, the link between incomes and prices is so close that the subject cannot be entirely evaded.

The *desirability* of an incomes policy is easy to prove. Briefly, an increase in wages not only adds to costs in the industry granting the increase, but also adds to effective demand and, particularly if wage increases are granted in several industries, makes it easier for the increased costs to be passed on in the form of higher prices. Incomes since the war in Britain and in most other countries have tended to rise faster than output, and also faster than prices.

If there is high unemployment, an incomes policy, in the sense of holding down incomes in any industry below the equilibrium level, has a good chance of success. Even if labour in that industry is by some criterion underpaid, it may not be able to leave. Employers have no incentive to undermine an incomes policy by open or disguised wage increases (fringe benefits, imaginary up-grading schemes, incentive schemes, payments in kind, better working conditions, subsidized sports and canteen facilities) in a time of recession. However, as the main aim of a prices and incomes policy is to permit national output to expand (*i.e.*, to make heavy unemployment unnecessary) while damping down the rise in prices, the fact that an incomes policy can work in times of depressed demand is not a strong point in its favour.

Since there are fewer wage-determining bodies and fewer formal wage changes, the problem of *selecting* wages or wage claims for investigation and control is probably less serious than with prices. However, the problems of *enforcement* are just as serious, given the variety of ways by which an employer who wants to attract more labour can evade the prescribed wage limit, and the difficulty of using sanctions against workers, trade unions, or employers who contravene the regulations.

To succeed, an incomes policy must satisfy a number of conditions, each of which in itself would raise serious problems. The first condition—the object of the exercise—is that the annual rise in the wage bill must be kept within the pre-determined limits. Secondly, the policy must be such as not to prevent wages and salaries rising in industries and occupations which need more labour. In the short run, or in conditions of depressed demand, this may not be very difficult, but the longer the incomes policy is in operation the more difficult it will become. Thirdly, unless the existing distribution of income—both the share of wages in the national product, and the relative position of different groups of wage earners—is to be frozen, allowance has to be made for increasing the earnings of the lowest-paid workers. In parentheses, it may be remarked that there is often an anti-manual labour bias in incomes policies. This is because manual workers reach their maximum earnings soon after they start their working life, while salaried workers obtain almost automatic increases up to middle age or beyond. Also, it is easier for salaried workers to get pay increases by changing jobs, and perhaps to get concealed pay increases in the form of fringe benefits. To sum up, the fact that an incomes policy is, from the macro-economic standpoint, desirable, does not, unfortunately, mean that it is practicable.

Investigation of almost any wage structure or proposed wage increase may, as with prices, bring results of the "business efficiency" kind. Many of the Prices and Incomes Board's inquiries have done so. Demolishing commonly accepted criteria for wage increases may be very valuable. All the White Papers on the subject have stressed that increases in the cost of living should not be regarded as justification for wage increases. While trade-union acceptance of an incomes policy may depend on a reasonable degree of price stability, it is certain that *if* the cost of living rises, this must not be regarded as a justification of wage increases; otherwise the inflationary spiral will remain automatic and self-perpetuating. Another formerly widely used but almost totally misguided criterion for pay increases is "comparability". The fact that workers in industry *A* have received a pay rise is no reason why workers in industry *B* should have one, if there is no shortage of labour in industry *B*; though the notion of fairness is so deeply embedded in wage negotiations that comparability will probably never be entirely eliminated.

Historical experience lends support to an adverse view of incomes policy in the sense of all-embracing and detailed pre-determination of wages. In the closing years of the 1945–51 Labour Government the wages policy of the period came near to collapse (admittedly because of exceptional price increases during the last few months of the period). The National Institute of Economic and Social Research has estimated that in the years 1965 to 1968 incomes in Britain rose by about the same amount as they might have been expected to rise given the prevailing level of unemployment, if no incomes policy had existed. In Holland, where wages policy was most fully developed, there was a breakdown in 1964, and in Sweden in 1966. A feature of the collapse of the Dutch wages policy was that its temporary success in the preceding years made the gap between Dutch and German wages wider, leading to large-scale poaching of Dutch labour by German employers. Like depression, inflation can only be effectively combated on an international scale.

The most comprehensive survey to date on the subject of incomes policies has this conclusion:

> . . . such policies, as so far conceived, have not proved strikingly effective instruments of economic management. The policies have achievements to record, but limited and temporary achievements. This does not mean that incomes policies are permanently doomed to ineffectiveness in market economies. But it does mean that if incomes policies are desired, the conditions in which they can be expected to operate successfully have not always been achieved.[2]

With this verdict we may leave incomes policies, hoping that they may be more serviceable in the future than they have been so far.

During the years when there was intensive discussion of prices and incomes policies in Britain—1964 to 1968—the view rapidly gained ground that the aim should be to allow prices to rise in order to "mop up" excess demand while holding down incomes. This view is set out, for example, in an editorial in the *Sunday Times* of May 28th, 1968, and in practically every issue of *The Economist* during these five years. This school of thought holds that all price increases are *de*flationary, and all attempts to hold prices down below the level they would otherwise reach is inflationary. (Nobody would dispute that price increases as a result of increased indirect taxes are deflationary, provided they are not followed by successful wage

[2] United Nations Economic Commission for Europe, *Incomes Policies in Post-war Europe* (Geneva, 1967), p. 1.

demands on cost-of-living grounds and provided the government does not spent the proceeds of the increased taxes.)

At first sight impossibly paradoxical, *The Economist*'s reasoning has some validity in terms of pure economics. A price increase "mops up" a certain amount of purchasing power, and holding prices below the level they would otherwise reach results in a certain amount of purchasing power remaining in the hands of consumers and being available to spend on other things, so adding to effective demand.

Apart from the political point that trade unions and professional organizations can hardly be expected to desist *indefinitely* from wage demands if prices continue to rise, the "mopping up purchasing power" view on closer inspection involves a number of fallacies. When the price of a product rises the extra money must be paid out to shareholders in the industry whose prices have risen, or paid out to workers. If it is put to reserve or ploughed back in the form of new investment, the shareholders still gain in the long run, and the payment is merely deferred. (For this reason dividend limitation is meaningless.) Similarly if a proposed price increase does not take place, consumers have more to spend but workers and shareholders in the industry which "has not" raised its prices have less.

More important, methods such as those discussed in the preceding chapters are designed to change the supply and demand curves for individual products, so that analysis based on fixed supply and demand is inapplicable. More generally, if the assumption in Chapter 1 is correct, preventing prices from rising forces entrepreneurs to look for more efficient methods of production, which are often available. (It is on this assumption that the management consultancy profession bases its operations and its success.) In such cases there will, again, be more goods and the same amount of purchasing power.

Consumer information is designed to increase the elasticity of demand for products which currently have inelastic demand curves owing to consumer ignorance. In these cases, less will be spent on the product in question after its price has been raised compared with the amount which would have been spent on it in the original state of consumer ignorance, but more will be spent on substitute or competing products. The net effect on the total amount of purchasing power available for spending on other goods and services (outside the group of competing products) should be neutral.

The argument that prices should be allowed to rise while incomes are held steady also neglects the effect of higher prices on the balance of payments, one of the main reasons for having an incomes policy. Price increases have an adverse effect both on exports (by reducing the competitiveness of domestic goods in foreign markets) and on imports (by increasing the competitiveness of foreign goods in the home market).

It might, indeed, in the long run turn out that one of the most effective means of implementing an incomes policy is *via* a prices policy, rather than vice versa. If prices are held, wages cannot rise very much as employers in the industries concerned will not have the money to pay higher wages. But if pressure is put in the first instance on wages, allowing prices to rise, then employers will make large profits, creating an incentive for trade unions to press their wage claims as well as enabling employers to grant them—especially if they are short of labour. As mentioned, there are innumerable ways in which employers can circumvent purely legal wages restraint which is not backed by any economic sanctions or pressure, though admittedly they will only want to do this in time of labour shortage.

The inter-relationship between the "micro" and the "macro" economic levels is, however, still rather obscure, and there may be cases in which *The Economist*'s line of argument is valid. If so, successfully preventing a price increase may have to be accompanied by higher taxation to "mop-up" the excess purchasing power. In the long run, a successful prices policy would probably result in higher savings by individuals, and the problem should become more amenable. Certainly it has to be recognized that neither prices nor incomes can be restrained indefinitely if the other continues to rise— a successful prices policy would tend to hold down incomes, as argued above, but if despite this incomes continued to rise, the prices side of the policy would break down sooner or later—for "demand-pull" as well as "cost-push" reasons.

Earlier, we argued that an incomes policy should not consist primarily of imposing pre-determined limits on wages and salary increases; and prices policy should not consist mainly of examining individual price increases to see if they are justified. Better to focus on policies for fighting price rises of the kinds discussed in Chapters 6 to 10, plus the "business efficiency" aspect of the Prices and Incomes Board's operations mentioned in Chapter 11. In other words our attention should be fixed on policy measures, not individual prices or wages.

The important things are breaking supply bottlenecks, the alternatives available to consumers, and the obstacles which prevent consumers from switching demand automatically from products which have risen in price, rather than the internal economics of the firm or the industry. The latter approach cannot bring out fully the alternatives open to consumers and therefore often turns out to be a blind alley.

While investigation of individual price increases may not be very fruitful (apart from their "business efficiency" aspect), investigation of *broad sectors* of consumers' expenditure would often throw up some useful policy suggestions.

There is little doubt that in clothing and footwear, furniture and other consumer durables, consumer information is the policy measure which would bring the largest economic gains. This leaves (1) fuel and energy, discussed in Chapter 9 and also in the present chapter; (2) transport, which poses special problems, though it was remarked in Chapters 8 and 9 that the long-term aim should probably be decentralized employment to reduce the demand for transport for "travel to work"; (3) a variety of miscellaneous goods and services; and (4) the two largest items in the consumer's budget, food and housing.

Potential economic gains from consumer information in food buying are mainly due to price differences at the retail level. Any other measures to prevent food prices from rising, or reduce them, would have to be of a different, mainly "political", character. In almost all countries the price of food at the farm gate is politically determined, in the sense it could be reduced by a political decision on prices, production or imports[3] (except in the case of the lowest-cost producers, such as Australia, New Zealand, and Denmark for temperate zone foodstuffs). Although the price of food at the farm

[3] This is not the place to discuss in detail the merits of different kinds of agricultural support systems. The British system relies mainly on subsidies to producers and allows prices to consumers to find their own level, while the Continental-type system relies on import controls and high prices to the consumer. The merits of the British type of support are that it does not reduce consumption, and has beneficial social effects. Even if the taxpayer and the consumer are increasingly the same person, food expenditure takes up a larger share of the incomes of the poor. It is sometimes claimed as an additional benefit of the British system that it keeps the cost of agricultural support "visible", but this is more doubtful. A survey carried out for the National Farmers' Union in 1963 showed that most people were aware and appreciative of (comparatively) cheap food in Britain, but few had any idea of the size of the subsidy bill.

gate accounts for only about half the price to the final consumer, the difference between the production prices of the lowest-cost producers and other countries indicates that there could be substantial price reduction in most countries if imports from the lowest-cost producers were increased.

Housing might be regarded as a politically influenced price in a different sense. A large and increasing share of total housing costs is made up of the price of land, which in turn depends heavily on the location of industrial and commercial activity. Location is influenced by many kinds of government action. In Britain the "land problem" basically concerns only the South-east and the West Midlands; in other large cities fairly small-distance shifts of industry and population ("overspill") are probably all that is needed.

The land problem in this sense can be alleviated by diverting the expansion of industry and population away from the South-east. It can *only* be dealt with in this way, since no other measure would change substantially the underlying supply and demand conditions. Nationalization of building land, or land taxation, diverts income from property owners to the state, but does nothing to reduce prices to the consumer. Price control would to some extent, as with other commodities, reduce the supply (*e.g.*, of land for building, and remove the incentive to economize in the use of land where it is particularly scarce. Low-interest mortgages and 100 per cent mortgages, on which popular and political interest tends to focus, would (in the unlikely event of their being made widely available) increase house prices by raising effective demand while doing nothing to change the supply conditions, and must therefore, according to the criterion adopted here, be regarded as against the consumer interest. As noted in Chapter 1, there is a particularly serious divergence of interest within the ranks of consumers, owing to the "investment" aspect of house-buying, so that a consumer strike—refusal to buy housing in areas where it is particularly expensive—must probably be ruled out.

The simplest and most effective method of reducing the rate of population expansion in the South-east would be a regional payroll tax. A measure of this kind, discouraging employers from setting up in particular areas but otherwise leaving them a free choice of location, has more to be said for it than inducements to employers to go to specified areas of high unemployment. A number of "physical" planning measures could usefully supplement a payroll tax. Military and naval installations in the South-east (Aldershot, Chatham,

Dover, Portsmouth) could be moved to other parts of the country and the considerable areas of land involved used for housing. New universities and research organizations should be sited outside the South-east (the expansion of London University since 1945 and the amount of residential accommodation thereby displaced would make a fascinating study). The proposed large new towns at Milton Keynes in Buckinghamshire, in South Hampshire, and at Ashford in Kent are highly unfortunate planning decisions, though the last now seems to have been abandoned. A further, if comparatively minor, measure would be to abolish the 45 per cent exemption from death duties attached to agricultural land, which would bring a disgorgement of land held mainly for tax-avoidance purposes.

Some final comments on the definition and selection of areas of intervention.

1. *Long-term price trends only should be considered*
In the long run scientific progress will change the nature of the problems facing consumers. Improvements in telecommunications should enable office employment to be decentralized, thereby solving at one blow the housing and transport problems of the typical metropolitan commuter. Area heating, fuel cells, and improved building methods should result from, and may reverse, the rise in the price of traditional fuels. But methods already to hand for dealing with rising fuel prices (such as cheap imports), or for dealing with housing and transport problems (such as stricter control over employment location), cannot be neglected on the grounds that in a decade or two science may provide new solutions.

The need to concentrate on long-term price changes (trends of at least a few years) is clear in dealing with food prices. A bad harvest will bring higher prices, but it would be misguided to put in motion long-term cost-reducing measures for this reason. It might be five or ten years before a programme of scientific research produces results, and it would obviously be wasteful to use this weapon against short-term price rises.

2. *Broad categories of consumer expenditure rather than individual products should be considered*
No serious harm is done by a rise in the price of one brand of soap, cigarettes, or biscuits if other brands' prices do not change. An increase in the price of all brands of soap, cigarettes, or biscuits is

a much more serious matter. Even more so is an increase in the price of all the items in one of the broad categories of consumers' spending—food, fuel, clothing, housing and transport. While the ratio of these to each other in consumer spending is by no means fixed—especially at a high standard of living—the fact remains that the individual consumer can easily use bargaining power against one firm in a competitive situation, but if the price of all the goods or services in one of these broad categories of expenditure rises, his power is very limited.

3. *The traditional but largely discarded distinction between necessities and other goods may be relevant*
Consumer spending other than on food, fuel and light, housing and transport (to work) can usually be postponed to some extent, and the "exploitability" of consumers in the residual areas (discretionary spending) is lower than where necessities are concerned. Not only are consumer durable goods substitutes to some extent for services, and vice versa, as noted in Chapters 6 and 10, but some commercially supplied services are substitutes for work which can be done by consumers themselves, and the existence of a second-hand market for durable goods imposes a further check on the ability of producers to raise their prices. Thus price-reducing intervention (consumer information apart) may need to be concentrated on food, fuel and light, housing and transport not only because these are probably of more "political" significance in the cost of living, so that an increase in price is more likely to lead to wage demands, but also because with other goods and services it is easier for consumers to take counter-action of their own.

These are only rough guide-lines. In the last resort, intervention must be concentrated where it is most likely to be successful and where the potential gains are largest. A research programme on the potential gains from different policies would be of great value, on the lines of the calculation of the gains from reduced obsolescence of automobiles quoted in Chapter 10. For example, the maximum potential gains from consumer information could be estimated from technical-economic information about the "value for money" of different brands combined with information about the brands' market shares; potential gains from import duty reductions could be estimated roughly by comparing foreign and domestic prices.

Such micro-economic measures, even if combined with more skilful use of macro-economic policies, might not halt the rise in the cost of living. Certainly there is little probability of this happening without a stabilization of government expenditure and a massive shift in taxation from taxes on income to taxes on expenditure.

Complete price stability, and still more stability in a particular statistical index, is unlikely, nor would it be desirable. Whatever base date is taken, the pattern of prices at that date is in some respects abnormal, and there is no reason why prices, any more than wages, should be frozen at the level prevailing at one particular time. Apart from the indispensable role of relative price movements, the possibility that a gradually rising price level provides a stimulus to economic growth cannot be ruled out.

However, it has been argued here that the fundamental reason for acting against price increases is not that they cause inconvenience to consumers, but that downward pressure on prices provides a stimulus to efficiency on the part of producers. After examining some possible price-reduction measures it was concluded that there are a number of these which consumers and governments have not used to the full. If an increase of 1 or 2 per cent per year in the cost of living is regarded as tolerable, the needed *reduction* in the rate of increase from the 3 to 5 per cent which has prevailed in Britain and most other developed countries under full employment is marginal; and policies such as discussed here, used together with macro-economic policies and a more fully developed incomes policy, might bring success.

Index